# Computer-Supported Decision Making
## Meeting the Decision Demands
## of Modern Organizations

# Contemporary Studies in Information Management, Policy, and Services (formerly Information Management, Policy, and Services series)

*Peter Hernon, series editor*

The Role and Importance of Managing Information for Competitive Positions in Economic Development
   *Keith Harman*, 1989
A Practical Guide to Managing Information for Competitive Positioning to Economic Development
   *Keith Harman*, 1990
Into the Future: The Foundations of Library and Information Services in the Post-Industrial Era
   *Michael H. Harris and Stan A. Hannah*, 1993
Into the Future: The Foundations of Library and Information Services in the Post-Industrial Era, Second Edition
   *Michael H. Harris, Stan A. Hannah and Pamela C. Harris*, 1998
Librarianship: The Erosion of a Woman's Profession
   *Roma Harris*, 1992
Statistics: A Component of the Research Process, Second Edition
   *Peter Hernon*, 1994
Research Misconduct: Issues, Implications and Strategies
   *Ellen Altman and Peter Hernon*, 1997
Service Quality in Academic Libraries
   *Peter Hernon and Ellen Altman*, 1996
Microcomputer Software for Performing Statistical Analysis: A Handbook for Supporting Library Decision Making
   *Peter Hernon and John V. Richardson (editors)*, 1988
Evaluation and Library Decision Making
   *Peter Hernon and Charles R. McClure*, 1990
Public Access to Government Information, Second Edition
   *Peter Hernon and Charles R. McClure*, 1988
Federal Information Policies in the 1990s: Views and Perspectives
   *Peter Hernon, Charles McClure, and Harold C. Relyea*, 1996
Statistics for Library Decision Making: A Handbook
   *Peter Hernon, et al.*, 1989
Understanding Information Retrieval Interactions: Theoretical and Practical Implications
   *Carol A. Hert*, 1997
Reclaiming the American Library Past: Writing the Women In
   *Suzanne Hildenbrand (editor)*, 1996
Libraries: Partners in Adult Literacy
   *Deborah Johnson, Jane Robbins, and Douglas L. Zweizig*, 1991
The National Research and Education Network (NREN): Research and Policy Perspectives
   *Charles R. McClure, Ann P. Bishop, Philip Doty, and Howard Rosenbaum (editors)*, 1991

## In preparation:

# Computer-Supported Decision Making
## Meeting the Decision Demands of Modern Organizations

by
Charles L. Smith, Sr.

Ablex Publishing Corporation
Greenwich, Connecticut
London, England

*H* Copyright © 1998 by Ablex Publishing Corporation

Printed in the United States of America

**Library of Congress Cataloging-in-Publication Data**

Smith, Charles L., Sr.
    Computer-supported decision making : meeting the decision demands of modern organizations / by Charles L. Smith, Sr.
        p. cm. — (Contemporary studies in information management, policy, and services)
    Includes bibliographical references and index.
    ISBN 1-56750-356-X (cloth). — ISBN 1-56750-357-8 (pbk.)
    1. Decision-making—Data processing. 2. Decision support systems.
I. Title. II. Series.
T57.95.S58 1998
658.4'03—dc21                                                                 97-34022
                                                                                     CIP

Ablex Publishing Corporation          Published in the U.K. and Europe by:
55 Old Post Road #2                        JAI Press Ltd.
P.O. Box 5297                                  38 Tavistock Street
Greenwich, CT 06830                      Covent Garden
                                                        London WC2E 7PB
                                                        England

*For my wife Beth, my children Chuck, Laurie, and Randy,*
*and also for Devin, Jeremy, and Blake*

# Contents

# Preface

One of the tenets that most of us learn early in life is that defining a problem prior to attempting to solve it is a critical aspect of addressing important issues. Unfortunately, many people seem to omit this problem definition stage from their decision-making process. Moreover, few authors have attempted to understand this aspect of the decision process so that others might use this structure in making decisions.

The implementation of an issue definition process into a model that can be embedded in a computer system is the method chosen here to create a decision support system (DSS) that can be used to support modern organizational decision makers. With the flattening of organizations and the empowering of more employees to become part of the decision-making process, there is an increasing need for some sort of computer-assisted mechanism to help in the decision process.

Yet another aspect of this idea is that the behavioral considerations of decision making have been ignored by those who create and build decision support systems. Part of this omission could be due to the fact that cognitive scientists do not fully understand the mental processes that humans use in making decisions. But enough is known that the behavioral models now available can be embedded in a computer system to offer a capability to support decision making while considering the different elements of an individual's cognition.

By intertwining the behavioral characteristics and the technological considerations of decision making within a prescriptive model for computer implementation, a system can be devised that can offer the kind of support that modern organizational decision makers are seeking. The approach to computer-assisted decision making developed and explained here is largely dependent upon the cognitive sciences, mathematical sciences, and organizational studies of the past few years. By bringing these together, a novel model has been created that offers the possibility of providing the kind of support decision makers desire.

There is a tide of competitiveness rising across the sea of business. The issues faced by the business commanders of today are rapidly becoming more complex. Veritable seas of information are crashing down on organizational decision makers. As the environment is becoming more complex, it is getting tougher to discern the relevant information among the flood of available data. The demands for accurate, rapid decision making is impelling today's decision makers to wonder about the existence of some sort of job-preserving assistance.

Decision makers are often awash in political controversy as well as technical, economic, social, and legal considerations. Relief from this sea of troubles will perhaps come from a behaviorally responsive decision support system in the form of computer assistance that considers the decision maker's cognitive needs. However, the design of such a system must consider the needs of a variety of people with differing levels of experience, different thinking styles, different responses to stress, and desires for differing approaches to the decision process. These capabilities must be designed into the DSS in order for it to be of any real benefit to today's and tomorrow's decision makers.

In the final analysis, the ability of an organization to beat its competitors may depend on the availability of computer assistance that can effectively support and even spur innovation. Acquiring and using properly designed computer support for decision making may be the answer.

# I

# Understanding the
# Decision Process

# I

## An Overview of Decision Making

### MAKING DECISIONS

As members of modern society we all must make decisions about many of the things that we do. Nearly all of these decisions are rather mundane, such as deciding, "What do I want to wear today?" or "Should I have dessert with lunch?" On some occasions, our decisions can be burdensome and quite important, such as, "What house should we buy?" or "Which car do I really want?" Depending on our occupation and position, our jobs may require many important decisions, such as those made by fire fighters, criminal investigators, managers of a business or some aspect of a business, doctors, lawyers or judges, and government and military leaders. Because we, as human beings, must make decisions daily, it is important that we understand the decision process, at least at some level, assuming of course that we want to be successful decision makers. The better we understand the decision process, the better our decisions should be. This statement seems intuitively true, although the argument for such a case could get laboriously complex.

Because of the extension of decision responsibilities to more employees in modern organizations (Hammer & Champy, 1993), the decision-making process is becoming an important element in the operation of most organizations for nearly all individuals in the organization. This is the implication of the term "employee empowerment," which is now used by many authors, such as Stephen Covey (1991) and Tom Peters (1987). Thus, more individuals and groups within modern organizations will be confronted with decision-making responsibilities. Some skills for improved decision making are offered by Hale (1996). However, all of Hale's five

3

skills and many more can be presented to organizational decision makers through the use of computer-based support systems.

Some authors take the approach that the computer should be used to make the decision for the user. This method is called an expert system. There are many expert systems, such as those for assisting in medical diagnosis (Bouwman, 1983; Doessel, 1986; Shortliffe, 1976), but none seem to consider that the decision maker may simply want support, not automated decision making. Expert systems can be used as stand-alone systems that make decisions in all situations (particular to some specific aspect of an environment) or they can be used as a subsystem for making decisions in particular situations. It is the latter case that will be of interest in this book.

Although there are many different programs that depend on expert systems or neural networks, these kinds of "nonspecific programming techniques . . . are often inferior to more problem-specific algorithms for encoding, inference, and learning" (Moravec, 1995). What could be more problem-specific than having the user perform the process of issue definition and applying a resolution process to determine a preferred response to a current or predicted state? This is the basis of the approach presented here.

Another form of decision support system is the On-Line Analytical Processing (OLAP) system, such as DSS Agent (MicroStrategy, 1995a, 1995b). These systems are being developed primarily to provide access to large databases. The OLAP systems do not provide the kind of support needed for most organizational decision makers. Generally, OLAP systems are used for non-real-time decision making, and are particularly designed for the manipulation of data in large databases.

In contemporary organizations, support for decision making in high-velocity environments[1] is required to meet daily challenges (Eisenhardt, 1989). This support is potentially possible through the use of the increased capabilities offered by modern information technology (Huber, 1990) in the form of a decision support system (DSS). These systems can aid decision makers in efforts to acquire, organize, process, present, and use information for making decisions. DSSs have utility if they provide effective and efficient support that improves the results expected from a decision process.[2]

Peters (1987) describes the trauma for decision makers in attempting to meet the challenges of the chaotic modern business environment. The complexity and rapidity of modern decision environments will require, in some cases, a support system to assist in dealing with the information chaos. Peters briefly mentions management information systems (MISs), a restricted version of DSSs, but certainly the need for an MIS or a DSS[3] to support decision makers in dealing with chaos and complexity is clear. The proliferation of cheaper, more capable computers with digital signal processors that "humanize[4]" them (English, 1995), plus the rapid organizational decentralization and empowerment of individuals at the lower levels of organizations to act as they think best (but within organizational constraints), and the availability of huge amounts of information, implies the potential need for computer-based systems with a diagnosis capability to assist in ensuring proper decisions.

Business and government decision makers must deal with situations that are already complex, and most issues are getting more complex daily. Generic uncertainties such as economic uncertainty (e.g., the price of oil or wheat next year), technological uncertainty (e.g., rapid advances in computer and telecommunications technologies), competition uncertainty (e.g., software competition among companies worldwide), and consumer uncertainty (e.g., growing consumer options requiring just-in-time material for flexible manufacturing systems) are creating gross uncertainties in potential outcomes and choices, creating a new definition for the winners in our society.

How do we deal with all of these uncertainties when making business and government decisions? For well-structured issues, operations research methods can be used, such as decision trees (Raiffa, 1970) or linear programming methods, but more often issues are ill-structured.[5] Dealing with increasing uncertainty requires adding more information input[6] to the decision process. At every point in time, entropy increases. That is to say, there is an increase in disorder which requires additional information to describe the situation (Prigogine & Stengars, 1984).

Increasing disorder requires increasing information to explain and resolve situations in modern society. To deal with the increasing complexities and the need for more information to understand these complexities, a computer-assisted process is offered. This process allows the user to identify, acquire, and process that amount of information needed to define the relevant situation for this particular user (i.e., decision maker). This is the purpose of this book: to explain a behavior-oriented DSS that can provide the support needed by modern organizational decision makers to deal with the complexities of our dynamic environment. This DSS should be linked to a variety of databases and data sources, internal as well as external.

Acknowledging that unpredictability cannot be removed or even substantially reduced by excessive planning, Peters (1987) points out that innovation, "an inherently messy and unpredictable business," is the key to the success of business organizations (and government organizations also). A properly designed and constructed DSS may also be the answer to stimulating innovation, whether in organizations that are sluggish or ones that are already creative.

Although luck plays a role in the level of success people have in making decisions, understanding the decision process and the relevant environment in which decisions are made can be critical to success in business or government crisis situations. Again, this seems intuitively clear. One should not expect a person who knows little or nothing about the game of chess to be able to play chess decently. Therefore, why should one expect people who know little or nothing about the rules for quality decision making to make good decisions, especially in complex situations? A wonderful way to learn about good decision making processes is to have a computer-supported capability that assures the user of the appropriate processes needed to make good decisions, whether the user is a novice, competent, or expert about his organizational environment (Smith, 1992).

Unfortunately, following rules defined for a good decision process does not ensure that the ensuing decision will result in a good outcome. However, following and understanding good decision processes should improve the likelihood that the resulting choices and associated outcomes will be better than those determined using poor processes.

## THE DECISION PROCESS

A principal objective here is to offer a comprehensive explanation of the decision process, particularly the early stages. The entire decision process usually consists of the following activities:

- issue detection,
- issue definition,
- response identification, and
- response implementation.

These four actions can be decomposed into many more activities, but they explain the general decision process in a simple manner. The first two activities are called *diagnosis* or *situation assessment*. The last two activities are called *situation resolution*. Diagnosis can be defined as follows:

> Diagnosis, or situation assessment, is the process of observing an environment relative to some issue of importance, collecting data about the issue and the environment into which it is embedded, and processing this data to enable one to detect potentially significant changes, current or future, to identify the likely causes, and to define the issue in proper relationship to the environment.

Situation resolution can be defined as follows:

> Situation resolution is the process of identifying alternative solutions, analyzing and evaluating these alternatives so that poorer ones can be screened out and the remaining ones can be rank-ordered, and selecting the preferred solution and implementing this action.

In general, there is no clear dividing line between the process of situation assessment and the process of situation resolution. In some cases, the process of defining the problem immediately leads to an understanding of the problem's resolution.

Diagnosis constitutes detecting and defining threats or opportunities in our relevant environment. The relevant environment consists of those aspects of the world that tend to affect the decision maker in some way. If I am the owner of a dress factory, my relevant business interests would consist of women's clothing styles; the cost and availability of labor, dress fabrics, dress manufacturing equipment, manufacturing buildings, heating and cooling of these buildings, and so forth; the cost of buying and storing dress material and other needed items; the state of the clothing economy; and other such aspects of manufacturing and selling women's clothes. Whether it is raining or not, whether the New York Yankees win or not or even play this year, or the fact that there was an earthquake in remote Colombia today is likely to be of little or no interest to me.

Nearly all formal or normative decision analysis efforts are concerned with situation resolution, often to the neglect of situation assessment. The tacit assumption is that the user somehow knows the proper definition of the issue, or that it has somehow been provided. In reality, issues are often not properly defined. A clear issue definition is key to the determination of an appropriate issue resolution alternative. Thus, there is a need for a situation assessment process, amenable to DSS implementation, that can be used to support various approaches to issue resolution.

Some researchers who have recognized this need for a formal approach to situation assessment or diagnosis for specific areas are Wohl (1981) for U.S. Air Force tactical decisions, Bouwman (1983) in the financial area, and Shortliffe (1976) and Doessel (1986) in the medical area. Computer-supported situation assessment can have beneficial effects. Gallupe and DeSanctis (1988) found that problem descriptions were significantly better in a DSS-supported environment than one which did not have DSS support.

Diagnosis is an information gathering and analysis process. Diagnosis can be used to assess the future, that is, to forecast future events based on existing and previous conditions. In the event of predicting or forecasting the future, a more proper term is *prognosis*. However, the same term, *diagnosis*, will be used here for assessing both current and future situations. Analysts try to anticipate the future by understanding the present (Naisbitt, 1984). Assessment of a situation is needed to identify the causal nature of changes that have occurred. A potentially challenging situation or issue will be diagnosed by identifying causal or symptomatic factors that explain the difference between the currently observed state and what would normally be expected at the present time, or what might exist at some future time.

A diagnosis process, to be truly effective and useful for supporting human decision making, must result in assistance that supports humans in accurately interpreting events in the environment. Computer-based situation assessment can be useful in recognizing complex issues that may require some sort of action. If an action is required, post-action situation assessment is also required to ascertain that the implemented action had the desired effect. Situation assessment assumes a dynamic environment that needs to be continually monitored for the occurrence of events of possible interest.

## WHAT IS AN ISSUE?

Issue detection consists of scanning the environment for data or information that indicates the possible existence of a situation needing attention. The process of issue detection or recognition usually requires a conscious process in terms of human monitoring efforts (Cowan, 1986). It is assumed that issue detection is generally a personal activity independent of the computer. The term *issue detection* will be used to represent the case of observing a change in the environment that may ultimately require some form of corrective action.

Inputs for the situation detection process may originate internally or externally to an organization from the observations by people and sensors (when appropriate), and all of this may be supported by databases, knowledge bases, model bases, or other forms of computer assistance. However, an appropriate definition of the issue may require computer support, particularly for complex issues. The information required to develop a proper definition of an issue should be kept to a minimum. This information can include data from personal observations (and could include gut feelings), newspapers, journals, magazines, TV programs, books, and so forth, or from information stored in relevant computer databases, perhaps on the Internet.

## WHERE DO ISSUES COME FROM?

Issues come about for a variety of reasons. A competitor introduces a new product, there is an increase in failures of an organization's product, or a computer at a bank suddenly fails: These are all examples of an issue. Issues are detected through some surge or sudden change to the relevant environment, through a series of small increments that accumulate to become significant, or from something in between these two extremes. A significant change to the relevant environment is a change (due to single or accumulated events) that makes a difference to the interested observer.

Because of our changing and increasingly complex environment, issues are becoming more difficult to define. The characteristics of modern organizations and our new environment, as derived from Peters (1987), are shown in Table 1.1.

The two columns are interdependent but the cross correlations are complex and the two columns should be read independently of one another. For example, organizations must be more responsive because of the changes occurring in the environment, such as increasing consumer demands and the demand for response timeliness.

## DEFINING THE ISSUE

Most people think that a *diagnosis* is what a doctor does when she is trying to infer the meaning, in terms of some understood disorder, of the maladies a patient is

**TABLE 1.1.**
**Characteristics of Modern Organizations and the Environment**

| Organizations | Environment |
|---|---|
| Flatter hierarchical management structure | Uncertainty |
| Increasing employee empowerment | Expanding emerging technologies |
| Increasing employee responsibilities | Expanding information availability |
| Service explosion | Increasing consumer demands |
| More responsiveness | Increasing foreign and domestic competition |
| More quality and cost consciousness | Increasing quality and option demands |
| Gain sharing | More choices |
| Increasing participation | Increasing demand for lower price and response timeliness |
| Values added through people | More complexity |
| Internationalist | More affluence |

complaining about. And by asking a proper set of questions of the patient (e.g., what, where, how, and so forth) and perhaps reviewing medical records, a diagnosis is performed. Unfortunately, diagnosis is an often overlooked aspect of all decision-making processes. Decision makers, whether in business or any other environment, are frequently ready to charge ahead by beginning the process of attempting to find a resolution to a problem they may barely understand. Very often, decision makers will discover that the problem that they have solved is not the true problem they should have been addressing. They have the option of admitting their mistake and formulating another set of solutions to the problem that they now feel that they understand, or ignoring the real problem and not admitting that they goofed. Inappropriately defining an issue is okay as long as the issue definition is rectified when feedback indicates an error has been made. But a primary objective of a DSS is to assure the user that an issue definition is accurate.

The complete decision process—that is, one that properly includes the diagnosis process—is generally not well understood by most decision makers. A principal objective here is to offer an explanation of the entire decision process, emphasizing both diagnosis and issue resolution of ill-structured problems.

Diagnosis can be thought of as an activity of attempting to understand what is going on at the present time so that a decision can be made to respond in some way. Or, diagnosis can be an activity for gauging the future[7] to ascertain if there is a need to consider some action later if one's prediction or forecast proves to be true. Acting on reliable diagnoses, or assessments, and forecasts can be essential in successful decision making in government, industry, business, and military environments. The better the current or future situation can be defined, the better will be the resulting decisions. This is because understanding the actual issue is basic to the process of creating a proper response. There is a notable exception to this rule. When there are only a few options (say, less than five), a rule such as "If situation is X, then respond with Y" may allow for the user to misdiagnose an issue X, yet sometimes correctly select the proper response Y. This is essentially a pathological case and will not be addressed further.

## DIAGNOSIS ERRORS

There are three types of errors that can occur in the diagnosis process:

1. Type I errors or missed opportunities (i.e., missing issues that should have been detected),
2. Type II errors or false alarms (i.e., detecting issues that aren't really issues), and
3. Type III errors that result from correct detection of an issue but an incorrect issue definition.

The first two errors can be addressed in a compensatory tradeoff manner by appropriately setting detection thresholds. The quality of information accuracy (i.e., Are the right parameters being used?) and precision (i.e., Are the data of sufficient detail?) are fundamental ingredients in determining Type I and Type II error probabilities. These types of diagnosis errors are usually associated with non-human systems and so are not of interest here. However, it is important to an organization that the human issue detection process neither frequently misses issues that should be detected nor frequently reports issues that are irrelevant or nonexistent. The determination of missed opportunities and false alarms is quite subjective and hence is difficult to do in most contexts.

To avoid Type III errors, a good definition of an issue is needed. The development of an issue definition process is one of the major objectives of this book. The use of different perspectives and models can assist in properly defining an issue. By viewing an issue from different perspectives, one can arrive at a more complete and improved issue definition (Allison, 1971; Etzioni, 1967; Linstone, 1984).

Diesing (1962) suggests that there are several perspectives that one might use to investigate an issue, namely, technical, economic, social, political, and legal. However, any perspective may be used as the decision maker deems proper, such as personal, organizational, and the views of pertinent others. In defining an issue, models are useful in building an understanding of the environment and events. Models also play an important role in analyzing the decision process and implementing a structured prescriptive model for the decision process.

## IDENTIFYING AND SELECTING RESPONSES

Once an initial definition of an issue has been ascertained (based on scanning information) and the user's stress has been appropriately assessed, the user must decide which decision strategy is proper for his particular stress level.[8] The basic alternative strategies are *rational* and *limited rational* decision making.

## Alternative Decision Strategies

Rational decision making is required for issues that are important and for which there is enough time for a formal decision process. Users are said to be rational if they select those options that are most likely to lead to the achievement of their goals. Generally, this involves multidimensional considerations, and there is no simple unique determination of rationality independent of the specific situation. Rationality is more complex than just considerations of a means-ends analysis, or input-output analysis, or optimization by maximizing a single scalar objective function. The forms of rationality, for example, those described by Diesing (1962), such as economic, technical, or social, act as constraints on the decision process by limiting the information required in the decision process. Rational decision making means using a structured evaluation method to identify and rank-order a set of alternative responses to an issue.

Limited rational decision making is for issues that are of limited importance and/or for which there is limited time, perhaps even very limited time, for assessing and responding to the issue. The user does not attempt to maximize some objective function, but instead tries to achieve some aspiration level. The aspiration level may change if the implied goal is either too easy or too difficult to achieve. Often long-range side effects are not addressed and changes are made in an incremental manner. Examples of limited rational decision making are Simon's (1972) "satisficing" (doing just enough to be responsive) and more specifically, Etzioni's (1967) "mixed scanning" (making incremental decisions and seeing if they work, changing the responses as required) or Lindblom's (1959) "muddling through" (making random responses and seeing if they work) decision strategies.

In the rational-actor model, the decision maker becomes aware of the problem, structures the problem space, collects information, identifies the effects of alternatives, and implements the best alternative based on a set of objective and subjective values. Since an exhaustive and complete list of every conceivable need—alterable, objective, and so forth—is not normally possible, one cannot in the classic sense of von Neumann and Morgenstern (1953) be completely rational in the purest unconstrained sense. These facts and the fact that people usually do not attempt to follow the prescriptions of the rational-actor model (because of cognitive limitations, time limitations, and information limitations) led Simon to define the satisficing decision-making process.

Other considerations in decision making are *risks* and *benefits*. Risk is the potential for harm or loss that might result from the outcome of a decision. Benefit is the potential for gain that might result from the outcome of a decision. For example, an investor might buy some stock at $100 a share but the price of the share might go down to $50 a share, resulting in a loss of $50 a share. That is the potential risk. Or the stock might go up to $150 a share, resulting in a gain of $50 a share. That is the potential benefit. The investor will usually consider the perceived possibilities of both the risks and benefits prior to purchasing a set of shares of stock.

Another consideration is *decision regret*. Decision regret is the amount of grief that may be felt by making a decision. Often decisions are made too early using inadequate information, or too late because of excessive information collection. The grief caused by a quick but less accurate response, provided it was an over-response, may be minimal, if any. This is the case with fire-fighting decisions. On the other hand, a very accurate but late response may result in a decision that has been overcome by events prior to its implementation. Decision regret is quite personal. That is, given the same conditions, one decision maker may feel extreme anxiety about making a decision, whereas another person may feel only slightly nervous or not anxious at all. Also, decision regret seems to be something that may be of more interest to an observer after the fact, rather than something to be considered during the decision-making process itself. However, the user should be aware of the timeliness requirements of a decision during the decision process so that a limitation is placed on the amount of supporting information that is gathered. The effect of decision regret perhaps can be considered when deciding among alternative options (Sage & White, 1983).

### Identifying the Alternative Solutions

Depending upon the decision strategy selected, there may be just one alternative to be developed. No matter how many options are developed, the user must be able to create one or more response actions that will resolve the issue. This process will depend on the user's ability to create responses that relate to the issue as defined during diagnosis.

### Selecting the Preferred Alternative

The manner in which the preferred alternative is selected can make use of methods for eliminating the poorer alternatives and methods for rank-ordering the remaining alternatives. These are explained in chapter 4 and in Appendix A.

## COMPUTER-SUPPORTED DECISION MAKING

Computer-assisted decision making and, in particular, computer-assisted diagnosis, is needed to meet the increasing demands on business, government, and military decision makers (Bouwman, 1983; Doessel, 1986; Huber, 1990; Shortliffe, 1976; Wohl, 1981). Varying levels of acceptance have been obtained with DSSs. Inadequacies are often due to difficulty of use, lack of user-friendliness, and a narrow range of typical applications (Ford, Schmitt, Schechtman, Hults, & Doherty, 1989).

However, advanced, highly capable computer systems are cheap and plentiful and with properly designed software can provide intelligent, inexpensive, and powerful support to decision makers (Andriole, 1986).

The situation is improved when decision support system designers incorporate interface considerations so that (a) the complexity of the domain is appropriately captured, and (b) this representation is effectively communicated to the user[9] (Rasmussen & Vicente, 1989). A user-friendly DSS should support a variety of user behavioral characteristics and needs. This requires that designers of support systems consider behavioral issues, as well as technological issues, in developing a DSS design concept. A DSS should consist of a human-computer interface that accurately and simply conveys the information in the computer to the user, and the user's desires to the computer. The DSS should also have a capability to manage information, whether in the form of data or models. A simple illustration of a basic DSS is shown in Figure 1.1.

The creation and use of DSSs will become increasingly important to decision makers because of the increasing complexity and rapidity with which responses must be made. Modern business and military environments present complexities that mean that many decisions are required in situations that are unfamiliar to even the most experienced decision maker. Thus, in these situations, even domain experts may be novices. Moreover, decision makers will be subject to different levels of stress during the decision process. This means that the architectural design of DSSs should include user-friendliness considerations to both *this user's* experiential level and potential stress conditions on *this user*. The emphasis of *this user* is added because each user has a personal experiential level based on the task contingencies of familiarity with the environment, the particular situation, the computer system, and the alternative decision processes, as well as personal feelings of stress due to the importance of the decision, time until the decision must be made, and other factors such as irreversibility of the decision, importance of the decision to significant others, and so forth.

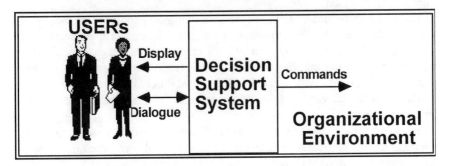

FIGURE 1.1. A simple view of a decision support system design concept.

There is a continuing need for improved capabilities to assist in individual and organizational decision making. The processes and interfaces presented here are derived to facilitate user comprehension of the situation, of alternative methods for gathering information, of alternative processes for defining and resolving detected issues, and of planning and implementing preferred actions.

The airline clerk at the check-in counter in any large airport in the world will use a sophisticated, but very specific, decision support system to make sure you have reservations on the flight of your choice (assuming that seats are available) or to confirm that you have a reservation, that you are assigned a specific seat on a specific flight, and that any special meal requirements are noted. Normally, this process is quick and reliable. In the future, more managers and employees will have personal computer (PC) systems on their desks. This PC or DSS will enable the user to collect data on the relevant environment, present this data to the user in an appropriate form (for this user), provide assistance in defining the issue if it is not familiar to the user, and assist in formulating, evaluating, and interpreting alternative options to resolve the identified issue.

These same DSSs will also be capable of providing the training needed to assure that employees are properly educated to handle their responsibilities. It should also assist them in creating, testing, evaluating, and finalizing new ideas to improve the organization's quality and responsiveness in its products and/or services. Peters (1987) states that employee empowerment means granting more decision responsibilities to lower echelon employees, often even including nonmanagerial people. This means that in the future more employees will have decision responsibilities. Organizations will become flatter, that is, the vertical tiers of management will decrease and company hierarchies will become more horizontal.

In the future, success will come to those who love chaos (Peters, 1987), but dealing with disorder will require improved structured decision processes that can be embedded in a DSS. The expanded use of DSSs will enable empowered users to thrive in a chaotic environment. This will be so because decision makers will be supported in their efforts to gather and evaluate data in a behaviorally relevant manner (to each specific user). Using DSSs will be fun and exciting to use because they will be designed to be enjoyed.

Only when it becomes fun to use the DSS will most people within the organization wish to use the DSS to assist in making decisions. This concept of an enjoyable DSS can be accomplished by being creative in the design of the interface screens and assuring that the DSS design meets the needs of real users. One approach to this is to provide the DSS with the capabilities to respond to the different needs of users with varying levels of experience, different biases, and different levels of stress.

Because of these changes in the environment and within organizations, the demands for organizational decision makers to respond to ever-increasing complex situations are depicted in Figure 1.2. Naisbitt (1984) says that "The computer will smash the pyramid." Those who continue to view organizations as pyramidal or

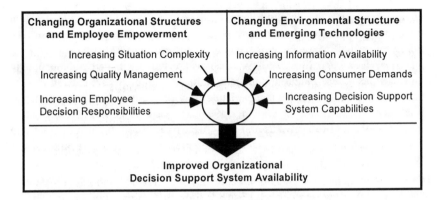

**FIGURE 1.2.   Meeting organizational decision-making demands in the 21st century.**

complex hierarchical structures have an incorrect image of the modern organization of the future, which must streamline to be competitive in a modern society (Peters, 1987).

The decision process described here is prescriptive. It blends the normative and the descriptive. It is not axiomatic, however, since theories and lemmas which can be mathematically proved or disproved are not being proposed. Nor is it purely empirical, since our conclusions concerning the worth of the process are not totally based on empirical evidence. Thus, it is a prescriptive approach which, when implemented, is capable of being embedded in an operational computer system.

There are support systems for groups of decision makers called group decision support systems (GDSSs). These systems are nothing more than a DSS for groups with a separate DSS monitor for each member of the group, perhaps with two displays, one for personal use and another for a public screen that all members can see and respond to. Members may be distributed, both spatially and temporally. If they are in the same room, then a single public screen can be used for all members to see. However, GDSSs are beyond the scope of this book.

## DECISION PROCESS MODELS

*Normative models* of decision making have logical and axiomatic properties. They describe a "best" decision in accordance with an axiomatic set of postulates. This generally results from maximizing a utility function that is based on several objectives or attributes. A decision maker who obediently follows these models is called "technically rational." Normative models typically deal with issue resolution in very idealized situations. The appropriateness of normative models is judged on the basis of mathematical elegance, parsimony (i.e., brevity), logical coherence, and philosophical coherence. Normative resolution processes assume that the decision maker understands the decision situation. The normative quantitative decision model most often used is based on the subjective expected utility theory constructs, initially presented by von Neumann and Morgenstern (1953).

*Descriptive models* illustrate how decisions are actually made by real people in real situations. These models are judged on the basis of predictive capability, face validity, and psychological insights. Three important descriptive models are (a) Janis and Mann's decision stress model (1977), (b) Rasmussen's cognitive control model (1980), and (c) Dreyfus and Dreyfus's five-stage human judgment and decision process model of novice, competent, proficient, expert, and master (1980).

*Prescriptive models* bridge the gap between normative analysis and descriptive analysis by prescribing how a real person in a real situation should realistically go about making a decision. A proper blending of the normative and behavioral models for decision making can result in a prescriptive model. Prescriptive models offer a structured approach to decision making through the use of defined steps that assure a proper decision process. Prescriptive models are amenable to implementation on a decision support system.

It is important that a DSS provide users who desire or need assistance in how to perform the decision process with an appropriate prescriptive model. The behaviorally-oriented model of a DSS as presented here is a prescriptive model.

## ENVIRONMENTAL MODELS

Models assist people in understanding some particular entity. There are three types of models for understanding the environment and the embedded events that the decision maker needs to comprehend, namely:

1. *purposeful* (What are the objectives of the situation elements?),
2. *functional* (How are the situation events being accomplished?), and
3. *structural* (What physical aspects of the environment are being used?).

An example of the three models is shown in Figure 1.3 for the case of a person who decides to drive to the grocery store to buy some groceries and return home. The reason (why?) I drive to the store (to buy some groceries) is described using the purposeful model. The manner (how?) in which I get to the store and obtain the desired groceries is described in the functional model. The objects (what?) that I use to get to the store and to gather the groceries once in the store are described in the structural model.

Purposeful models represent the hierarchical intents that may be achieved by the environmental process being monitored. These intents are the objectives of the process. Functional models describe the activities that are being used to accomplish the objectives described in the purposeful model. Structural models describe the

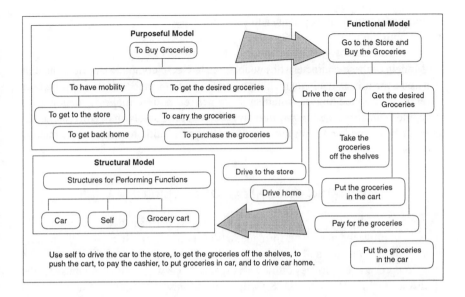

**FIGURE 1.3.    Sample case of purposeful, functional, and structural models.**

physical elements of the environment that are used to perform the functions or actions that create the situation as described in the functional model.

One important application for environmental models is for "What if?" analyses. These analyses are for investigating possible events that might explain the observed data. By modeling the environment, one can theorize possible explanations of the situation, simulate these explanations (i.e., the what-if situations), and compare the simulated situations with the collected data.

## BEHAVIORAL MODELS

Behavioral characteristics include the different elements of psychological processes used during human decision making. These elements include the intellectual, cognitive, and control skills often called "cognitive ergonomics" (Sage, 1992). Cognitive ergonomics as used here includes the following human attributes:

- user styles (viz., modes of thinking),
- levels of experience,
- levels of stress,
- human errors,
- biases (e.g., hindsight and overconfidence),

- judgment and choice options, and
- learning.

Models of these characteristics enable one to create computer applications that can assist the user in decision making by adjusting to the needs of the specific user. Over time, by tracking the manner in which each user makes decisions, the computer can form a *user profile* using behavioral models that will enable the computer to provide prompts and assistance that will facilitate the decision-making process.

## IMPROVING ORGANIZATIONAL PERFORMANCE

Organizations that can improve the decision-making performance of their employees will improve the overall performance of the organization. Because of the rapidly increasing complexity and availability of large amounts of data for input to the decision process, employees of modern organizations will need computer-assisted decision making. However, DSSs will be used only if they offer the benefit of improved decision making in return for a reasonable amount of time and energy, with minimal frustration.

Using the DSS should be fun; its design should be game-like so that users will actually look forward to using the computer to help them make decisions. It should be especially user-friendly, in a way that most computer applications are not. The user should not get frustrated while using the computer. Displays should be simple, yet meet the demands of decision making while providing the support that this user desires. The DSS should be sophisticated enough to provide even the most analytical users the support they expect while maintaining an intuitive approach for nontechnical users. This sophistication should be made transparent to the user.

## SUMMARY

A presentation has been made of the essential elements of the decision-making process with a background discussion of the increasing importance of accurate and rapid decision making in modern organizations. The ingredients of potential sources of error and considerations of decision risks and regret were presented. The importance of that portion of a decision process dealing with creating an accurate issue definition was stressed. Then a connection was made between decision makers and computer-based support mechanisms. Following this, a brief discussion of some software capabilities of models for describing the decision process, the environment, and human decision behavior was presented. The chapter concluded with a discussion of the organizational benefits that can be achieved through the use of computer-based systems to assist in making accurate and rapid decisions in response to a dynamic environment.

   As you read through this book you will find a certain amount of redundancy in the presentation of the material. The reason for this is that by repeating the concepts in different forms at different times throughout the book (i.e., using different perspectives), the reader will gain a better understanding than if these concepts were presented just one time.

# 2

# What Is Wrong With Human Decision Making?

## UNDERSTANDING OURSELVES

As human beings we have many fallibilities, such as *ignorance*, *pride*, and *fear*. Ignorance is simply a lack of knowledge about a specific area. No person is exempt from this limitation; however, some people do not wish to admit to ignorance, even about a specific issue. Pride is another human foible. Pride can be taking pride in one's capabilities; that is self-respect. But that is not what is meant here. What is meant is the kind of pride that causes arrogance or haughtiness. Fear can be another limitation on a decision maker. Fear can appear in many forms, but usually as some type of stress condition, such as a feeling of pressure due to time limitations or importance of the situation.

Many decision makers do not wish to be confronted with negative information about the lack of success of their decisions. This attitude can result in a decision maker making decisions that in some cases could cause great harm to his organization. Thus, it is important for a computer-based system to assist the decision maker in overcoming such a bias.

As Socrates so correctly stated, "Know thyself." By understanding our decision-making strengths and weaknesses, we can take actions to improve our abilities to make better decisions. As our business environments become more complex, the use of an appropriately designed DSS to assist in making use of our abilities and the access to information will become more urgent.

## Decision Record

A large part of understanding ourselves is knowing what our record is with regard to the success, or lack of success, in our decision making. If we know that some of our decisions were successful and some weren't, and we also know something about each decision, then we will be able to determine what we did when we made decisions with successful outcomes. In this case the user should strive to repeat those types of decision processes.

We can also know what we did when our decisions were not so good, that is, when the outcomes were less than ideal. In these cases we can, if good records were kept, know what we did wrong and make the proper corrections to improve our future decisions.

A recommended decision record format is shown in Table 2.1.

The decision record could include the following items:

1. date of the decision,
2. a brief description of the situation,
3. a brief description of the decision,
4. importance of the decision,
5. complexity of the situation and the decision,
6. outcome of the response action,
7. effect of our decision on the outcome,
8. our responsibility relative to the set of decisions required to select the response action, and
9. the decision process used.

## Describe the Situation

The situation should be described in as few words as possible, but making sure that the description is sufficient so that when the user goes back weeks, months, or even

### TABLE 2.1.
### Record of Personal Decision Outcomes

| | |
|---|---|
| Date | 7/12/96 |
| Description of situation | Sales falling, competitor introducing new product |
| Description of decision | Decided to create a new and more competitive product |
| Importance of situation | Very important |
| Complexity of situation | Very complex |
| Outcome | Good outcome, the new product regained company market share |
| Our responsibility | Partially involved, about 25% |
| Decision process used | Systematic approach; multivariate utility analysis |

years later, he will be able to understand what the situation was at the time it occurred.

Situations are either familiar to the user (or to the DSS, if automatic issue recognition is used) or unfamiliar. The different situations are shown in Table 2.2. A situation can differ from other situations based on whether it is important or not and whether there is sufficient time to make a formal deliberation or not. This means that the response to a situation should be created on the basis of the degree of importance and the time in which a response can be formulated, analyzed, and interpreted. If the situation is important and there is ample time for identifying a formal solution, then a formal response generation process can be followed. For a formal approach to creating an issue definition, see Appendix D. We will not be concerned here with such formality in defining an issue.

### Describe the Decision

The actual decision made by the user should be described. It should provide an understanding of the action that was recommended by the user.

### Decision Importance

The importance of the decision should succinctly describe the meaning of the decision to the organization. This meaning can be, for example, in the following categories: very important, important, average importance, unimportant, very unimportant. Remember that the user can provide whatever rating categories seem to fit his desires.

### Complexity of the Situation/Decision

The complexity of the situation can be based on the number of parameters that were used to describe the pertinent environment. Usually the more parameters it takes to describe a situation, the more complex the situation. Similarly, the more alternatives that must be considered as potential responses to a situation, the more complex the decision.

**TABLE 2.2.**
**Responses to Situations**

| Situation | Response process | | |
|---|---|---|---|
| *Familiar* | Known response is generated | | |
| *Unfamiliar* | *Situation is important* | | *Situation is not important* |
| | Limited time | Sufficient time | |
| | Informal response generation | Formal response generation | Informal response generation |

## Outcome

Since the outcome may not be known for weeks or even months, it is important that the user keep good records and return to the appropriate point in the table to record the outcome and the effects of the decision on the outcome. By periodically reviewing the table, the user can spot the table locations that need to be filled in when certain data are obtained.

### Effect of the Decision

The effect of the our decision on the outcome is usually subjective, but should be honest. This assessment conveys the relevance of the user's decision to the outcome. This effect may be difficult to ascertain, but the accuracy of the determination of the effect will influence the meaning of this particular decision.

### The User's Responsibility

Assess the user's responsibility relative to the set of decisions required to select the response action. That is, what proportion of the final response could be attributed to the specific decision from this user?

### Decision Process Used

The decision process used can be either intuitive or systematic. These will be explained later, but intuitive generally means that the selected response is based on experience and common sense. Systematic means that the selected response is based on a formal approach to formulating and evaluating the alternative responses.

### Record Summary

These recommended items might be accepted as is, or changed according to the beliefs and results that a particular decision maker has for using them. Decision makers should keep records that satisfy themselves.

In later chapters many of the aspects of the decision record presented above will be explained, such as situations, decisions, decision processes, and so forth, and the meaning of the decision record will become more apparent.


## THE INFLUX OF INFORMATION AVAILABILITY

In our modern information age, with personal computers on nearly everyone's desk; access to the multimedia Internet and many external databases, many internal databases, and sometimes a data warehouse or data mart; cable TV; newspapers, magazines, and journals; and other information sources (including our own senses), we are being bombarded with great amounts of information. How can we ever process even a small portion of this information? How can we identify the appropriate sources of information? How can we identify what is relevant? How can we gather and evaluate the information? People may not be able to do these things efficiently. A properly designed decision support system can provide the needed assistance.

## UNDERSTANDING THE ISSUE

Once an issue has been detected, or at least a perceived issue has been detected, it should first be properly defined. This is not a simple process for complex issues, because there are so many aspects and different interdependencies that most people cannot do this task mentally, at least not for problems that are complex or where there are many problems to be solved in a short period in a chaotic situation.

## THE ADVANTAGES OF COMPUTER-SUPPORTED DECISION MAKING

Even though many decision makers seem to be able to make good decisions without any computer support, the issues are getting more complex and the results of our decisions are becoming more meaningful, so that any assistance that can improve decisions should be used (Peters, 1987). A computer-based system can assist the decision maker in this process. The computer system can assist the user in the data gathering process for identifying an appropriate issue definition, in finding a solution to the issue, and even for implementing the solution, if the user so desires.

## INNOVATION IN THE ORGANIZATION

A key to the success of business organizations is innovation (Peters, 1987). Whether in identifying new products and services or new methods for business processes, innovation can enable an organization to succeed. And the lack of innovation can cause an organization to eventually become ineffective or even defunct.

## MAKING DECISIONS AMIDST CHAOS

Because of the rapidity of change and the increasing amount of information that is becoming available, most organizations are becoming inundated with both the amount of information and the need to properly process this information. In contemporary organizations, support for decision making in chaotic situations is needed (Eisenhardt, 1989). With the proliferation of communications system network access and personal computers, both desktop and portable, the availability of computer-supported decision making is rapidly becoming easier. However, executives, managers, and others will not resort to using computers for decision support unless the software becomes more adaptable to their behavior (Sage, 1992).

# II

## Understanding Computer-Supported Decision Making

# 3

## Creating a Personal Computer System to Help Make Decisions

### THE PROLIFERATION OF PERSONAL COMPUTERS

Personal computers are everywhere. They are on desktops and in briefcases. Connectivity of computers to relevant networks is becoming simpler and more prolific. However, software for assisting users in modern organizations to make high-quality and rapid decisions does not exist.

### WHY AREN'T SUPPORT SYSTEMS SIMPLER?

Most designers or vendors who create decision support systems tend to give little thought to including human behavioral characteristics in their system architecture. Including these characteristics is complicated and requires a better understanding of how a computer system can provide an adaptive mechanism to suit the different users who may use the system.

The general attitude towards the creation of a decision support system or any other programmed computer software system is that the user must learn how to use the system, not that the system should adapt to the user. The creation of a computer system that can adapt to the user requires both an understanding of how human beings think and behave as well as how computers can be embedded with the desirable attributes of decision technology and human behavior. The process of designing, developing, and producing the desired DSS is called a life cycle.

29

## A LIFE CYCLE PROCESS

A popular life cycle process for developing a DSS is shown in Figure 3.1, although there are many others, such as those for developing commercial products (Smith & Sage, 1989).

The entire DSS structured project life cycle process usually consists of the following sixteen phases:

1. initial requirements identification for DSS
2. concept definition
3. concept development
4. prototype development
5. prototype test
6. prototype demonstration to client
7. use of prototype to identify user DSS requirements based on client involvement
8. use of requirements to identify DSS specifications
9. preliminary design of the operational DSS
10. detailed design of the operational DSS
11. coding, unit testing, debugging, and integration testing
12. computer software component item testing
13. system integration and testing
14. overall DSS testing and evaluation
15. demonstration of operational system to the client for approval or feedback
16. finalization and modification for final DSS software package with concomitant documentation

At any point in the life cycle process, the manager will likely wish to iterate back to an earlier phase. The classical management POSDCORB functions can be used to properly manage the life cycle process as defined above (Sage & Palmer, 1990).

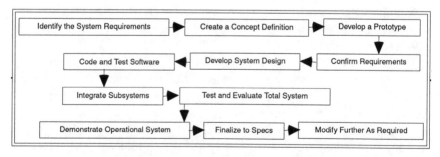

**FIGURE 3.1.  A popular life cycle process.**

The POSDCORB functions are planning, organizing, staffing, directing, coordinating, reporting, and budgeting, and are defined next.

*Planning* involves identifying the environment of the organization, identifying objectives or goals, developing policies, determining courses of action, making decisions, setting standard operating procedures and rules, developing programs, forecasting future situations, preparing budgets, and documenting project plans.

*Organizing* involves identifying and structuring required tasks, selecting and establishing organizational structures, creating organizational positions, defining responsibilities and authority, establishing position qualifications, and documenting organizational structures.

*Staffing* involves filling organizational positions, assimilating newly assigned personnel, educating and training personnel, providing for general development, evaluating and appraising personnel, and making and documenting staffing decisions.

*Directing* involves providing leadership, supervising personnel, delegating authority, motivating personnel, developing standards of performance, establishing monitoring and reporting systems, measuring results, initiating corrective actions, and documenting all of these.

*Coordinating* involves coordinating activities, facilitating communications, resolving conflicts, and managing changes.

*Reporting* involves documenting decisions and preparation of informational reports such that there is appropriate awareness of the organization's activities. In a more general context, it involves developing information resource management capabilities and implementing these in the organization.

*Budgeting* involves the determination of financial and accounting strategies to ensure that the organization has the ability to carry out its mission.

A quality assurance process can be used to assure that the life cycle process steps are properly performed and completed within budget and scheduled timelines with the highest quality, based on the assignments of appropriate personnel. Total quality management can be incorporated throughout the process by assuring that a proper relationship is maintained with the identified user requirements and the product of each life cycle phase.

The particular life cycle process appropriate for DSS development depends on whether the client needs a single system unit, several units in the system, or a large network of many distributed systems. In the latter case, the designer may wish to consider developing an architecture for the network.

The descriptions of the three subsystems of a DSS (Sprague & Carlson, 1982)—dialogue generation and management subsystem, model base management subsystem, and the database management subsystem—are presented next.

As shown in Figure 3.2, every DSS comprises three parts, the first being a dialogue generation and management system (DGMS), which provides display presentation to, and dialogues with, the user. The DGMS provides a linkage to the other two parts of the DSS, the database management system (DBMS) and the model base management system (MBMS) (Sprague & Carlson, 1982).

The DGMS is responsible for producing DSS output representations, for obtaining the user inputs that result in the operations on the representations, and for interfacing to the memory aids for explicit provision of the control mechanisms that enable the dialogue between user input and output and the database and model base management systems (Sprague & Carlson, 1982). Database management must be capable of coping with a variety of data structures, such as flat files and relational or object-oriented data. One purpose of the database management system is to support the model base management.

The most important characteristic of model base management is that it should enable the user to explore the situation through the use of the databases by a model base of algorithmic procedures and management protocols that allow the DSS user to extract knowledge from the data in the database management system. Other desirable attributes of model base management are that it should (Dolk, 1988; Geoffrion, 1989)

1. *provide multiple models* to accommodate user needs for flexibility;

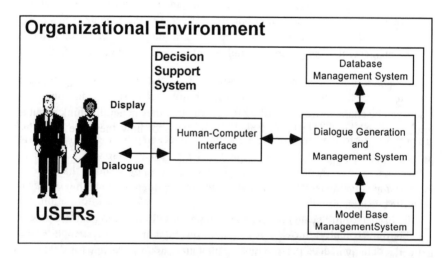

FIGURE 3.2.   A decision support system design concept.

2. *provide an on-line capability* to access, create, modify, validate, execute, and store models; and

3. *provide three types of bases*, personal (for access by each particular user only), semi-personal (for access by the user and selected others), and public (for access by anyone), in a group context.

A primary objective of the DSS concept presented here is that human behavioral characteristics should be embedded in the system to ensure true user-friendliness (Smith, 1992).

## HUMAN BEHAVIOR CONSIDERATIONS

Human beings are subject to the limitations and variations of their cognitive capabilities, which reside in each person's mind. A person's problem-solving capabilities can be modeled based on the following: knowledge level, cognitive style, alternative modes of reasoning, creativity, biases, alternative decision-making processes, decision stress, and learning.

### Knowledge Level

Users will have varying levels of knowledge about the environment in which they operate (Rasmussen, 1980). Some users will have a great deal of knowledge and will be referred to as "experts." These are users who have much experience in the relevant environment. Some users will be experienced but will not be experts. These users will be called "competents." Some users will be new to the environment or will find the issue a novel one that they have not ever seen before. These users will be called "novices."

Note that the level of knowledge is based on the particular issue being addressed, so that even a so-called expert may be a novice for some issues. Thus, the DSS should offer alternative methods for resolving an issue to all users at all times.

### User Styles

Users can be characterized according to the way that they generally think about an issue. A user's style can be modeled on the basis of how they like to collect information and how they like to evaluate the information. User styles can be divided into two categories, information gathering and information evaluation.

*Information gathering* relates to the processes by which the mind organizes the diffuse stimuli it encounters, rejecting some of the information, and summarizing and categorizing the rest. Gathering can be divided into preceptive and receptive thinking. *Preceptive thinkers* bring to bear concepts to filter the data and focus on relationships between items and look for deviations from, or conformities with, their expectations. Precepts (i.e., data categories or trends) act as cues for cataloging the data they find. On the other hand, *receptive thinkers* are more sensitive to the stimulus itself. They focus on detail and try to derive the attributes of the information from direct examination of it (McKeeney & Keen, 1974).

*Information evaluation* refers to the problem-solving process. Evaluation can be divided into systematic and intuitive thinking. *Systematic thinkers* tend to approach an issue by structuring it in terms of some method that will lead to a solution. However, for certain tasks they can develop a method of procedure that utilizes all their experience and economizes on effort. Conversely, *intuitive thinkers* tend to use more solution testing and trial-and-error methods. They may jump from one method to another, discard information, and be sensitive to cues that they may not be able to identify verbally. They are better able to approach ill-structured problems, where a large volume of data, the solution criteria, and the nature of the problem prohibit any predetermined method (McKeeney & Keen, 1974).

It is convenient to use a personal profile for modeling a user's approach to decision making. A personal profile is a model of the user's psychological abilities to gather and assess data. The personal profile can be embedded in a DSS and can be used to provide the user with suggestions for data gathering, issue identification, and issue resolution. The personal profile can be determined in at least two ways: by the user or by the DSS. Users who understand themselves can provide the DSS with a description of themselves. The DSS can accumulate a personal profile by identifying the user's actions with regard to data collection and decision making. As the DSS gathers these data, the data can be stored in the personal profile as a description of the user's cognitive personality. Still another way is to let the user create an initial personal profile but then allow the DSS to gradually modify it based on the user's actions.

Whatever the user's style, he must decide on the appropriate mode of reasoning with regard to a specific issue.

**Modes of Reasoning**

There are three models of reasoning about an issue: induction, deduction, and abduction. An understanding of these approaches should assist the decision maker when trying to decide on the proper approach to defining and resolving an issue.

There is no mode of reasoning that will always assure the user of reaching the true answer. Whatever conclusions are reached based on some collected facts (whether they are actually true or not), the conclusions are really hypotheses and are not known for sure; it is only likely that they are true.

The creation and evaluation of hypotheses can be based on any form of reasoning. Three forms of reasoning and their uses are described as follows:

- *induction* is the process of inferring a hypothesis based on the accumulation of evidence, and represents going from the particular to the general;
- *deduction* is the process of identifying data that must exist for an assumed hypothesis to be true, and represents going from the general to the particular; and
- *abduction* represents the analogical generation of alternative hypotheses or the possible existence of data based on scant evidence, and represents an imaginative or creative approach that identifies the existence of hypotheses or data when there seems to be little evidence to suggest either.

An example of induction is the following. Suppose we enter a friend's apartment and see that it is in a terrific mess. It is known that just hours earlier, the room was tidy. It is also known that there have been reports of burglaries in the area. By *induction*, an inference is made that there has been a burglary of this apartment. An example of *deduction* in this case is concluding that the apartment has been burgled but additional data are needed to support the inferred conclusion. We decide that if it has been burgled, it is deduced that the person who lives in the apartment would not know that the apartment is in a mess. We call the person on the phone and ask her to describe the condition of the apartment. The tenant answers that the apartment is tidy except for a cup of coffee on the table in the kitchen. We assume that the tenant is giving an honest answer. This response tends to confirm our hypothesis of a burglary.

Abduction requires much knowledge of the situation and was used by the fictitious character Sherlock Holmes created by Sir Arthur Conan Doyle. Actually, it was Charles Sanders Peirce (Schum, 1987) who realized that there was another form of reasoning other than inductive and deductive.

In the same case as above, we see that the apartment is in a terrific mess and abductively conclude that there has been an attempt by the tenant to cause the police to believe that the apartment has been burgled, and that it is very likely that something of great value will be found to be missing. This conclusion is based on facts that we know: the tenant is in grave financial condition and has a record of having been involved in lawlessness previously. Through questioning of the tenant we find that an expensive painting is missing. We later find that the tenant took this painting she had bought recently, sold it to a dealer in another city, faked the burglary, and claimed that the painting had been stolen so she could collect the insurance, which was in the full amount of the painting's value.

The use of any one or all of the reasoning methods should be used when attempting to generate the alternative issue definitions. If there is sufficient time and desire on the part of the user, then the list of alternatives should be mutually exclusive and reasonably exhaustive. However, many users, especially those who are expert in the relevant environment, will feel the need to generate only a single hypothesis. Competent users will tend to generate perhaps two or three alternatives and novices may seek to generate an exhaustive list. This means that competent and novice users will be the most likely to benefit from the more formal aspects of a DSS. However, for very important issues and when there is sufficient time, even expert users may wish to use the systematic approach offered by a DSS.

Some knowledgeable people are quite good at abductive reasoning. Since the decision maker is an integral part of a user-DSS system, that system has an abductive reasoning capability to the extent that the user has that ability. Abductive reasoning is required to create alternative hypotheses and conceive alternative solutions to the developed issue definition, especially for an intentional system[10] where issues and resolutions may not be readily definable using inductive and deductive reasoning.

Abductive and deductive reasoning can also be applied to the information acquisition process. The information desired can be defined, ranked, and selected as a miniature situation assessment. Then the best source can be determined, and the information can be accessed or elicited, and appropriately debiased and weighted, or discounted, prior to entering it into the evidence set. Once entered, the information's contribution should be properly assigned to any hypothesis that it affects. The type of new information desired is affected by the kind of inquiring system[11] being used.

By combining the different methods of reasoning with the alternative inquiring systems, the user can identify issue definition alternatives using a structured prescriptive process that is amenable to DSS implementation.

*Using induction.* Induction is a logical process of going from the collected evidence to inferring a hypothesis of the issue (particular to general). That is, what must have been happening in order for the facts that I have gathered to have been the case? Thus, induction is a "collected data imply some particular situation" approach.

*Using deduction.* Deduction is the process of examining the conjectured issue definition and deciding that certain additional data must exist (general to particular). If this additional data is collected, the additional data can be used to determine that the conjectured issue definition must be true. Thus, deduction is an "issue definition implies data to confirm or disconfirm" approach.

*Making like Sherlock Holmes.* Conan Doyle's famous sleuth Sherlock Homes may be the best known user of the abductive approach to solving a mystery. Abduction is the use of a set of facts that are generally insufficient to clearly define and resolve an issue. This process makes use of the known facts to conjure up a plausible issue definition, or to identify the possibility of missing facts, or to ascertain one or more potential issue solutions. It is an inside out approach to using some known facts to theorize both the definition of the issue and the potential issue resolution. Abduction therefore is a "gathered facts imply the issue, or other facts that have not been found as yet, or a potential solution" approach.

Abduction is very dependent upon a person's knowledge about the pertinent environment. It is this knowledge that can stimulate a person's abilities to identify issue definitions, needed facts, or potential solutions when the available information appears to be insufficient to do such a thing. It means making the most of the situation and requires creativity and ingenuity. It is an ability to read much more into the available facts than might normally be observed.

To properly apply a reasoning process, the decision maker may require a process for stimulating creativity.

## CREATIVITY

Many decision makers need an environment that fosters the process for creating alternative issue definitions, a list of additional relevant facts, or alternative solutions to an identified issue. Methods for doing this are called *idea generators*.

Idea generators such as brainstorming, forced relationships, attribute listing, morphological analysis, synectics, Delphi, and others can be used to stimulate abductive (or analogical), deductive, or inductive creativity in the users for generating ideas relevant to some objective (Evans, 1989; Sage, 1977). Three of the more popular forms of idea generation are brainstorming, morphological analysis, and Delphi.

*Brainstorming* is probably the most popular of the idea generation methods. Brainstorming requires that an individual

- identify the basic issue,
- identify as many alternatives as he can think of, even if it may seem silly,
- not criticize the potential contribution of any alternative,
- continue until he runs out of ideas, and
- when a set of ideas has been generated, sift through them and screen out the poorer ones.

Iterate through the process as many times as desired until the number of alternatives is believed to be satisfactory.

For issue generation, brainstorming is a process that consists of

1. identifying as many possibilities as come to mind, without regard to the quality or sensibility of each,
2. creating a list of these possibilities,
3. evaluating these to see which ones are promising,
4. pursuing the remaining items,
5. examining the alternatives to see if they are mutually exclusive and appropriately changing or eliminating those that are not correct, and

6.  examining them to see if they are exhaustive and identifying any new ones that may be needed.

*Morphological analyses* are oriented toward creating a structure to illustrate the different dimensions and possible relationships of the attributes of an issue. Morphological illustrations are usually in two and sometimes three dimensions so that they may be viewed to assist in understanding the issue.

For example, suppose the user is interested in transportation alternatives in a rural area. The options are horse, horse and buggy, car, and truck. The attributes of these options are purchase cost, miles per dollar, number of riders, speed, terrain requirements, luggage capacity, and maintenance requirements. The attributes can be quantified and qualified in tabular form as shown in Table 3.1.

The morphological structure could have been presented in three dimensions (see Figure 3.3) using transportation mode, efficiency, and effectiveness, where efficiency includes purchase price, miles per dollar, and maintenance; and effectiveness includes speed, terrain, number of riders, and luggage.

*Delphi analysis* involves asking experts (people who have a great knowledge about the relevant environment) to study an issue and present their collective opinions. Then the user can assess the issue based on some sort of consensual impression given by the group of experts. This approach has the advantage that the user gets other people to do the analysis. If the quality of the Delphi membership is high and the analysis results are such that all members are in general agreement, then the analysis results can be highly credible and useful. Problems can occur when time is limited, cost is limited, finding an appropriate Delphi group is difficult, and the Delphi members do not consensually agree on the issues, or when the expertise of the Delphi members is subject to question.

**Biases**

There are people who will base a decision on a particular fact or supposed fact such as something they recall in an apocryphal story they may remember. For example, they may recall the following story:

TABLE 3.1.
Morphological Structure for Rural Transportation

| Mode | Price | Miles/Dollar | Speed | Maintenance | Terrain | Number of riders | Luggage |
|---|---|---|---|---|---|---|---|
| Truck | high | 15 | 60 | medium | roads | 3 | lots |
| Car | high | 30 | 90 | high | roads | 6 | some |
| Horse | very low | 10 | 5–10 | low | all | 1 | little |
| Horse & buggy | low | 10 | 5 | low | roads | 2 | some |

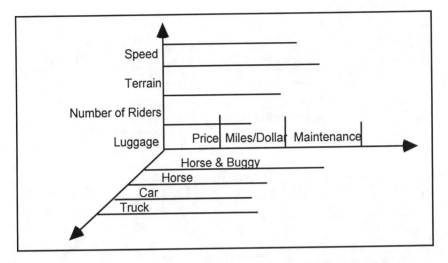

**FIGURE 3.3.   Morphological structure.**

A driver is traveling at 90 miles per hour and runs off the highway and hits a tree. The car explodes, but because the driver is not wearing a seat belt, he is thrown clear of the car and lands in a farmer's haystack unharmed. Had he been wearing his seatbelt he would surely have died in the exploded car.

This person will ignore the easily available statistical information on millions of accidents where the lives and bodies of drivers and occupants are saved because they were wearing seatbelts and where drivers and occupants were killed or maimed because they were not wearing seatbelts.

By understanding that we are subject to such biases, the decision maker can make a conscious decision to gather objective data and logically evaluate the information. By presenting the user with a set of potential biases, the user can take the appropriate action to avoid any biases that they know they may have. Many biases are listed in Appendix C.

**Decision Stress**

Janis and Mann (1977) have developed a decision stress descriptive model that can be used to prescribe the appropriate decision process in response to the various levels of user time-stress. It implies the type of situation assessment required for a decision maker at the various levels of conflict defined in the theory, as shown in Figure 3.4.

Janis and Mann feel that three of the coping models are potentially appropriate: unconflicted adherence, unconflicted change, and vigilance. Two of the coping

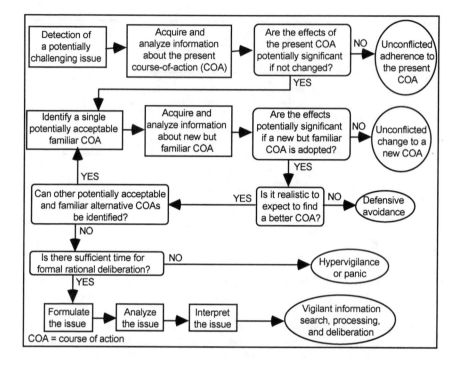

FIGURE 3.4.   Janis-Mann decision-stress theory model.

levels are maladaptive: defensive avoidance and hypervigilance. However, the vigilant level can be inappropriate if there is a time-stress constraint on the user. Janis and Mann state that the two primary contributors to decision stress are potential losses (risks) and gains and the effects on the decision maker's reputation. They also state that their decision stress model is driven by these three contributors:

1.   risks,
2.   hope for finding a better solution, and
3.   available time to find a solution.

Since the DSS can provide assistance in finding a better solution using the prescriptive model and the alternative interfaces, the remaining stress contributors are risk and time.

The context of the Janis and Mann model is a single individual who is faced with typical decision situations. However, in an organizational environment, decision makers are faced with multiple decisions, some near simultaneously, often creating a crisis environment.

In this time-stress-based decision-stress theory context, a descriptive model of situation assessment consists of the following activities:

1. evaluation of general input information to recognize that there is a potentially challenging threat or opportunity;
2. requesting additional information about the situation effects if the present course-of-action (COA) is continued;
3. requesting additional information about the situation effects if a change is made to a new, but familiar COA;
4. requesting additional information to ascertain if it is reasonable to find a better COA than the familiar COAs already considered and dismissed;
5. requesting still more information to ascertain if familiar COAs not previously considered are acceptable;
6. requesting information concerning whether the remaining time until the decision must be made is sufficient for a formal rational deliberation; and
7. requesting information to support a formal formulation, analysis, and interpretation of the issue with a vigilant search, processing, and deliberation.

An important use of this model in DSS support is to assist the user in such tasks as

- gathering information that can indicate the improper continuation of the current COA, or proper or improper change to a familiar COA; and
- understanding defensive avoidance and hypervigilance situations through enhanced awareness of situations and potentially providing a limited rational decision strategy alternative to enable the user to quickly resolve a high stress situation.

There are alternative processes or models for making decisions. These are described next.

**Models of Decision Making**

There are several models of decision-making processes. It is useful to know these alternative methods to ensure that the proper one is being used or that an improper one is avoided. Once an initial definition of an issue has been ascertained (based on scanning information) and the user's stress has been appropriately assessed, the user must decide which decision strategy is proper for his particular stress level. The basic alternative strategies are *rational* and *limited rational* decision making.

*Rational decision making* is required for issues that are important and for which there is enough time for a formal decision process. Users are said to be rational if they select those options which are most likely to lead to the achievement of their goals. Generally, this involves multidimensional considerations, and there will be no simple unique determination of rationality independent of the contingencies created by the specific situation. Rationality is more complex than just considerations of a means-ends or input-output analysis and optimization to maximize a single scalar objective function (Diesing, 1962). The form of rationality selected for choosing among alternative responses tends to act as a constraint on the decision process by limiting the information required in the decision process.

*Limited rational decision making* is for issues that are of limited importance and/or for which there is limited time, perhaps even very limited time, for assessing and responding to the issue. The user does not attempt to maximize some objective function, not in an essential way, but instead tries to achieve some aspiration level. The aspiration level may change if the implied goal is either too easy or too difficult to achieve. Often long-range side effects are not addressed and changes are made in an incremental manner. Examples of limited rational decision making are Simon's (1972) "satisficing" or "bounded rational decision making." and more specifically, Etzioni's (1967) "mixed scanning" or Lindblom's (1959) "incrementalism" decision strategies. Below is a discussion of some of the decision models that have been identified.

*Rational-actor model.* In this model, the decision maker becomes aware of the problem, structures the problem space, collects information, identifies the effects of alternatives, and implements the best alternative based on a set of objective and subjective values. Since an exhaustive and complete list of every conceivable need—alterable, objective, and so forth—is not normally possible, one cannot in the classic sense of von Neumann and Morgenstern (1953), be completely rational in the purest unconstrained sense. These facts and the fact that people usually do not attempt to follow the prescriptions of the rational-actor model (because of cognitive limitations, time limitations, and information limitations) led Simon to define the satisficing or bounded rationality decision-making process.

*Satisficing or bounded rationality model.* Bounded rationality appears when the decision maker implements decisions on the basis of a minimum set of requirements to provide a threshold of acceptability in the short term (Simon, 1972). The decision maker does not attempt to optimize an objective function but attempts to achieve a defined lesser level of acceptability. The level of acceptability or threshold may possibly change because of difficulties in searching for a solution or from lowering or raising the threshold depending on extenuating circumstances (i.e., too easy or too difficult).

*"Muddling through" model.* The decision maker attempts to respond to opportunities by avoiding bold changes to the status quo based on a somewhat

limited set of alternative courses of action, which amounts to minor perturbations to existing policies and rules (Lindblom, 1959). Long-range effects are ignored, thereby leaving them to future decision makers who will probably try to mitigate these issues with other incremental decisions. Often people use the muddling through process when they understand neither the problem nor a proper approach and simply make a sequence of minor decisions and see what the effects are after each one, making corrections as they go.

*Mixed scanning model.* The mixed scanning strategy is defined as the efficient use of a low-risk decision process. Etzioni (1967) says that the most effective strategy is the one that is most well-suited to the specific situation and to the decision maker's capacities. This is the essence of the robust mixed scanning model. The mixed scanning process consists of examining the situation and one's available resources for responding, then responding incrementally while scanning the environment to see how the response is working out, and then continuing the selected action, modifying the action, or changing to a different action if the scanning indicates such. Decisions are made so as to optimally use the available resources.

Etzioni believes that his mixed scanning strategy allows for greater realization of goals than either incrementalism or rationalistic approaches because the incremental use of input information with contextual decision making provides for both short-run probing of alternative courses of action and long-run criteria for evaluation.

*Organizational processes model.* When the standard organizational policies or rules are effectively communicated, each member of the organization is aware of the standard operating procedures for responding to certain situations. Decisions, if desired, can be made and then adjudicated based on these standard procedures. Required information for making decisions is defined in terms of how these standard operating procedures or rules were used in prior problems. Standard operating procedures should be a minimal set so as to allow decision freedom to the users.

## Human Error

One of the purposes of a well-designed DSS is to avoid human errors. Errors may exist both in situation assessment and in situation resolution. Reason (1987) describes three basic types of cognitive control error: slips, lapses, and mistakes. *Slips* are failures in execution or unintentional actions. *Lapses* involve mental forgetfullness. *Mistakes* are due to the selection of inadequate approaches so that the desired outcome is not achieved. A goal of the DSS for situation assessment is to minimize the number and effects of these slips, lapses, and mistakes. The interface should allow the user to recover easily from these errors, that is, to rectify slips, to remember important items, or to mitigate mistakes.

One potential way to diminish human error is to allocate a portion of effort that might be performed by a human to the DSS in the hope that this will lessen the cognitive load on the user. Two environmental or domain contexts, *familiar* and *unfamiliar*, and two occurrence possibilities, *anticipated* and *unanticipated* events, are of importance. *Familiar domains* are those where the DSS user is experienced or where experience has been stored in the knowledge base of the computer. In these domains, it is possible that support models have already been developed and prestored for automation of effort. The DSS can be programmed so that an expert subsystem can be designed to identify and resolve familiar issues.

*Unfamiliar domains* are those in which the user is inexperienced, and where no DSS experience base is available. Therefore, support models must be defined and constructed. Figure 3.5 illustrates a conceptual model of this task allocation.

In allocating some of the workload to the computer, Rencken and Durrant-Whyte (1993) have developed an algorithm that automatically allocates tasks between a user and the computer. In their study it is assumed that the computer can always perform the assigned task in a satisfactory manner. However, this may not always be possible. The issue may not be recognized by the DSS, for example. In this case, allocating unfamiliar issues to the expert subsystem in the DSS is a distinct possibility. Of course, the expert subsystem will be unable to respond properly in this case.

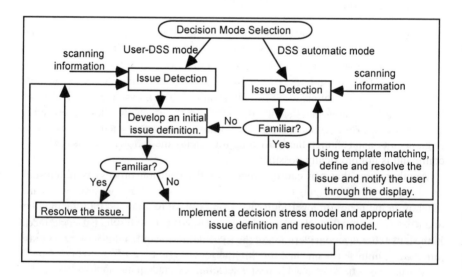

**FIGURE 3.5.   Issue allocation to user or DSS.**

Therefore, their algorithm needs to be modified to handle cases where the DSS may not recognize issues. With this accomplished, it would be possible for the user to allocate all situation assessment and resolution tasks, for which the DSS has an embedded and experienced knowledge base, to the DSS. The user could then personally respond to those issues for which the DSS (i.e., the expert subsystem) does not have experiential familiarity.

When the DSS is selected (automatic mode), familiar issues (to the DSS's expert subsystem) can be automatically detected and resolved by the DSS based on template[12] matching (Noble, 1987). In an environment and situation where several issues and their many different tasks[13] are observed and performed concurrently, a likely occurrence in many organizations, a user may wish to have some low-priority situation assessment and resolution tasks assigned to the DSS in order to alleviate cognitive loading on the DSS user. This would allow more time and effort for high-importance issues. The tasks assigned to the DSS should be those which the DSS can perform accurately and properly.

Many human errors might be ameliorated either by improved training or through better interface design (Rasmussen, 1986; Rasmussen & Vicente, 1989). Many human errors result from two important causes. Errors may result from either

1.  problems with the domain models or the prescriptive rules, or
2.  a misunderstanding of the displayed information.

These sources of error imply that user-friendly interfaces should either minimize the effects of human errors or allow for correction when the errors occur. The interface can accomplish this by displaying information in a manner appropriate to the user's knowledge level or thinking style. Since some errors cannot be eliminated, they must be handled through error recovery or correction provided by a proper interface design.

Slips and mistakes do not necessarily require modifications to the support system to be corrected. They usually require that the issue definition and resolution process be repeated from some earlier point. Slips can sometimes be detected by the DSS, such as when a user command violates a domain functional model's constraints (e.g., laws of nature), then the DGMS might display the following message "This command is not physically possible."

Another error that can cause a repeat of the decision process is if unusual sensitivities of some outputs to some inputs are discovered. Some sensitivities are inherent in the nature of a particular issue and cannot be changed, or they may be due to the manner in which certain dependent variables were selected or defined. In the latter case, a reconsideration of the issue definition or resolution process may remove or diminish the unusual sensitivities.

Should the user feel that support requirements are not being met, based on feedback, then changes to the DSS should be implemented. These causes of error include

1. changes to a familiar environment that make the environment somewhat different from before;
2. use of the DSS in a new and unfamiliar environment;
3. occurrence of an unanticipated situation that requires an update of automatic issue detection templates and support models;
4. changes in the organization's standard operating procedures or, alternatively, limitations in the standard operating procedures that require modifications, deletions, or additions;
5. changes in the organization's goals; and
6. changes in the user's support requirements.

**Learning**

At the end of the situation assessment (and situation resolution) process, if there is sufficient time, one should evaluate the process to ensure that the various tasks were performed properly and comprehensively. This can be accomplished by using dialectic questioning of the procedures and performing a sensitivity analysis. In essence, the user must question the decision process and examine its capability to provide the desired and needed support. If there are any errors in the DSS process, the user should detect, identify or define, and appropriately correct them.

There are at least three basic options for employing a learning mechanism to change the DSS to suit the users:

1. maintain a single DSS that is modified on the basis of consensual agreement among all the users of this DSS,
2. maintain a separate DSS for each user so that each user can modify his own system to suit his specific needs, or
3. maintain both a basic DSS for use by anyone in a group of users, and a separate DSS for each user.

In the second and third cases, the individual system is private and cannot be accessed without the password of the individual user. Probably the third alternative would be preferred, since it allows for a reference system that each user can use and examine for ideas, in addition to an individual private system.

A most efficient learning process is based on Argyris's (1982) organizational learning model (see Figure 3.6). This prescriptive model involves questioning currently implemented organizational (or personal) decision theories in an effort to detect, define, and resolve errors in these theories.

This process is called double-loop learning and corrects *slips* and *mistakes* by repeating some task or procedure, or it may involve modifying the currently implemented DSS-supported decision process. This dialectic, or *deutero*, learning (Sage, 1990) can occur as a result of two categories of error in the decision process:

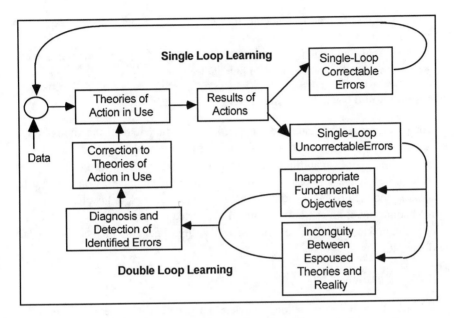

**FIGURE 3.6.   Illustration of double-loop learning.**

1. errors detected during the decision process, and
2. errors detected by valid but imperfect feedback information after the issue definition or resolution implementation has been completed.

The different types of system modifications are

1. changes[14] to the standard operating procedures or other information in the model base or database, such as new production rules for template search;
2. changes to the database when data seem to be inappropriate;
3. changes to models in the model base, particularly the situation assessment prescriptive model and familiar situation templates; and
4. changes to the dialogue generation, model base, and database management systems, such as new or modified screen presentation capabilities, e.g., modified menus, altered icons, and improved picture presentations.

## TECHNOLOGY CONSIDERATIONS

The design of a DSS must consider the alternative technological capabilities that can be used to deal with the human behavioral aspects of decision making.

Technology considerations include the various technologies incorporated into computer and network systems, asking the proper questions when attempting to define an issue, and attempting to understand how to design a computer that can respond to the behavioral aspects of human decision making.

## Computer and Network Technologies

Computers are getting faster and cheaper, and the commercial off-the-shelf (COTS) software is becoming much more capable of dealing with the needs that people have. Multimedia capabilities offer alternative methods for getting information from the computer and providing information to the computer. Computers offer desktop and laptop devices so that whether a user is at work in his office or on the road somewhere, he can have computer-supported decision making. Laptops for decision making are dependent on the availability of network connections to data or people.

## Asking Questions

Usually, the initial information for a detected issue will involve any or all of the gamut of possible questions, namely, who?, what?, when?, where?, how?, and why?, and the many variations of these questions. For example, given that something has occurred and has been detected, an interested observer might begin by attempting to get answers to the following questions about the general situation:

1. Who is involved, generally?
2. What is occurring, generally?
3. When did it happen, generally?

In unfamiliar situations, this information can be used to form an initial issue definition. To form an additional set of information for a more formal issue definition, the user needs to establish a set of appropriate questions for which the answers will provide information for developing alternative issue definitions (i.e., hypotheses). Basic information may be provided by most any source, such as key observers or reference material. However, further information may be required.

Following in a manner similar to Wohl (1981), the questions are stated and the responses are given in the context of a fire ground commander assessing an urban fire situation:

1. *What is involved, generally?* (A building is on fire.) Determine the physical structures that are involved in the detected occurrence. The answer requires information concerning a general description of the physical structures involved in the issue.

2.  *What is occurring, generally?* (A police report says that a building is on fire.) Define, in general terms, the event(s), or symptom(s), that is (are) occurring. The answer will require observations concerning the nature of the disturbance.
3.  *Where is the occurrence, generally?* (The building is near the corner of Elm and Main streets.) Determine the general location(s) of the event(s). The answer will require observations or information concerning the location of the environmental disturbance.

The information required to answer these first three questions should be contained in the original set of observations. These observations are the values for a set of parameters that are monitored for any indications that a relevant event has occurred. The answers to a basic set of questions will give a general idea of the event. Further questions must be formulated and answered to get a better concept of the issue. For the case indicated, some additional questions are listed as follows:

4.  *How is it occurring?* (A mathematical, or functional, model can explain the physical laws of a fire.) Determine the physical and/or procedural processes by which the event is being accomplished. Purposeful, functional, and structural models must be created if not already existing (with a model base manager) and/or used to explain the structure and dynamics of the detected domain issue.
5.  *When did the event begin?* (Using data and a mathematical model, one can estimate when the fire began.) Determine the approximate time of the onset of the event or symptom. This is often required to properly use the functional model. It also may indicate the appropriate required response. In some cases, the time of event onset may not be of interest, or it may not be determinable until after some other questions have been answered.
6.  *What is occurring, specifically?* (The fire may be composed of chemicals and other highly flammable material.) A more specific description of what is occurring will likely require more information than that provided by the initial detection scanning vector. The answer to this question will require detailed information that should be of value in forming, testing, and modifying hypotheses.
7.  *Where is the occurrence, specifically?* (The fire may be confined at present to the first floor. Ensure that the fire is not composed of multiple separate fires located around the building.) Determine the specific location of the event. Human observations or sensor data must supply information indicating where the occurrence is. The detection information itself may give a good enough indication of the specific location. However, a search of the entire domain may be necessary to ensure that all events of interest are located and identified. This thorough search may be performed using some efficient search algorithm or heuristic rule. If an efficient heuristic rule is available, it can be used for either user-learned rules or as stored rules for automatic search algorithms, which can be used to guide the user.

8. *Who is involved?* (There may be people in the building.) Determine the people who are involved in the occurrence. If anyone is inside, they may need assistance evacuating the structure. For many issues, this may not be a pertinent question. Other people may be involved. For example, if the situation is an arson fire, then we will need to identify any information that might indicate who may have started the fire. Perhaps it was started unintentionally.

9. *Why is it occurring?* (The fire may have been accidentally started.) For an unintentional event, this question may not make sense because the person who caused the event did not have any intention to do so. For intentional events, one needs to determine the probable objective for the perturbation (the detected event) to the environment. That is, if this is an intentional event, what is the possible objective of the instigator?

This is a recommended order for, and list of, appropriate questions in a particular domain, namely fire fighting. In other environments, a different set of questions would probably be more appropriate. If an appropriate set of questions can be identified for a particular environment, then they can be programmed into the DSS so that these questions are addressed to the user by the computer, if that is desirable.

The DSS may also offer suggestions, such as a recommendation to access, modify, or build structural models that will enable the user to answer specific questions. The elicitation or acquisition of required information may be evaluated based on the potential benefit of the information as well as the credibility of the information source, and the cost and time required. Only information passing some sort of efficacy test may be acquired. The efficacy test might consist of determining the benefit of the to-be-acquired data in terms of the anticipated quantitative improvement in the plausibility or credibility of a hypothesis versus the time and cost of acquiring or eliciting the data. If this kind of test could be determined and used in such a way so as to not limit the user's abilities to define the issue, then this kind of approach would greatly diminish the acquisition of irrelevant data.

**Dealing with Human Limitations**

There are methods that can be used to deal with human limitations. For example, if a user is not knowledgeable about the current situation, then the decision maker can call on an expert system to make the decision, or at least to offer a possible decision. This of course assumes that there is a relevant expert for this issue. Otherwise, the user will have to resort to an evaluation method that allows for the decomposition of the issue resolution into parts which can be evaluated so that the alternative can be rank-ordered.

In the case of pride, it is hoped that a presentation by the DSS of what can happen when decision makers allow pride to affect their decisions may cause the decision makers to take actions that will diminish the effects of pride. Similarly, by predicting that the user may be under some stress, the DSS can offer a decision process that will serve to lessen the effects of stress.

*Expert subsystems.* In a decision support system, an expert subsystem can provide needed decision-making capabilities in situations in which the user does not have the appropriate abilities to make a decision or is time-constrained and wishes to off-load some of his decision responsibilities. An expert system is software that provides the decision-making capability of an expert in the form of decision rules or if-then statements. These statements attempt to replicate the decision abilities of a person who understands some aspect of the organizational environment. The decision rules are elicited from a selected decision maker and then transformed into computer software. An example of an expert system is shown in Figure 3.7. An expert system consists of a database, a knowledge base, and a rule interpreter or inference engine.

In an expert system, the *database* consists of parameter values that describe the current environment, where the environment can be described using the parameters $x_1, x_2, \ldots$ ; an environmental state is described when values for these parameters are known. For example, the state of a ballistic missile in flight can be described by its seven parameters, time, position, and velocity, of its center of gravity and the position and velocity are in a earth-centered inertial system. The *knowledge base* consists of the expert rules that express the different responses to domain conditions as shown in Figure 3.7.

The control scheme (or rule interpreter or knowledge engine) is simply a set of instructions that tell the computer how the expert rules should be executed. For example, the rule interpreter could be as simple as

Do rule i for i = 1 until rule i is true or until all rules are exhausted.

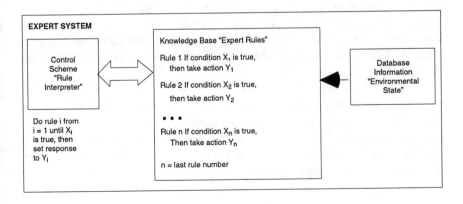

**FIGURE 3.7. An example of an expert system.**

*Dealing with biases.* There are two basic methods for the DSS to deal with human biases. One is simply to present a list of biases and warnings to the user, hoping that the user will recognize the potential application and seek to avoid the particular bias. Another is to use a personal profile of the user that indicates to the DSS that this user has a particular bias (or biases) so the DSS can caution the user and make the appropriate recommendations.

*Limited rationality.* When the user is subject to time stress, then the proper approach to resolving the issue may be a limited rational or satisficing approach. In this case, the DSS could recommend the alternative decision approach by asking questions of the user and inferring the stress condition based on the user's answers.

*Stress levels.* Because humans are subject to decision stress, it is important that the DSS be able to determine that the time restrictions and issue importance are such that either a satisficing approach or a formal rational approach should be recommended for appropriate decision making.

## User-Friendly Interfaces

Many potential users may seek to avoid the DSS if it is too difficult to use. Well-designed interfaces that are user-friendly will improve user attitudes towards the DSS.

Although most interface researchers recommend consistency, Grudin (1989) warns against attempting to be too consistent. Grudin states that "rejecting consistency as a primary user interface goal does not argue for randomness in user interface design." Thus, some sense of consistency is required but it must be placed in its proper context.

*Motif.* The latest technology in standardizing the development of human-computer interface capability is the use of Motif interface guidelines and the OpenGL de facto standard. The OSF/Motif style guide (Open Software Foundation, 1993) provides a framework of behavior specifications to guide application, widget,[15] user interface system, and window manager developers in the design and implementation of new products consistent with the Motif standard user interface. The style guide is closely consistent with Microsoft Windows, Presentation Manager, and Common User Access.

The style guide establishes a consistent behavior among new products by drawing out the common elements from a variety of current behavioral models. It anticipates the evolution of graphical user interfaces (GUIs) as new technology becomes available and as the use of Motif user interfaces spreads. Behavioral guidelines will be added over time as they become stable. The Motif guide provides some guidance concerning consistency when building a GUI.

Some of the Motif guidelines are the following:

1. Adopt the user's perspective by understanding what the user does and wants.

2. Give the user control by ensuring that applications are flexible and offer progressive disclosure, keeping interfaces flexible by providing multiple ways for users to access application functions, and providing alternatives such as pulldown menus, direct manipulation of objects, or a mnemonic key press.

3. Provide real-world metaphors by ensuring that push buttons need to be pushed and scales need to slide in order to work. Also allow direct manipulation, provide rapid response, and link outputs with inputs for subsequent actions.

4. Keep interfaces natural by making navigation easy, providing natural shading and coloring with appropriate contrasts, and using color as a redundant aspect of the interface.

5. Keep interfaces consistent so that as the user proceeds from one interface to another, the interfaces have the same behavioral aspects.

6. Communicate application actions to the user by giving feedback, anticipating errors by avoiding potential errors in the interface design, and using explicit destruction, for example, when an action has irreversible negative consequences, it should require the user to take an explicit action to perform it.

7. Avoid common design pitfalls by paying attention to details, not finishing with the interface design prematurely, and starting with a fresh perspective when designing the interface.

An approach that is gaining favor among most users is the use of multimedia interface designs. Multimedia is the use of visual (pictures or video), audio (sounds or messages), and other aspects of human senses such as touch (pressure and heat), smell, and taste for assisting in understanding and responding to situations.

*Other considerations.* The human-computer interface should be designed so that users with different stress levels, different modes of thinking and reasoning, and different experience levels can all use the DSS with ease.

# 4

# Behavioral Characteristics of Decision Making

## PRESCRIPTIVE MODELS

When decision support systems were first being developed, designers were not aware of the need to pay attention to who might be using them. The assumption was that the user must learn how to get the DSS to do what the user wanted it to do, using the interface and other aspects of the systems as they were designed. In other words, the users had to modify themselves to conform to the DSS. For this and many other reasons, people did not use DSSs, and, like other aspects of information technology, early DSSs were not accepted by potential users. Because of the trend in computer system user-friendliness, DSS designers have become much more aware of the importance of including behavioral characteristics in their DSS designs.

Behavioral characteristics include the different elements of human psychological processes. The elements that include intellectual, cognitive, and control skills are often called human factors engineering or cognitive ergonomics (Sage, 1992). Human factors were developed by cognitive scientists. "Cognitive science is concerned with the scientific study of mind, information, and intelligence. It has as its goal an understanding of how one can represent intentions, purposes, knowledge, and thinking in a physically realizable system, such as a person, animal, or computer" (McCain & Segal, 1988), or any combination of these. For example, a DSS user can be considered to be a human-computer system.

The cognitive aspects of decision making as used here includes user styles, levels of experience, levels of stress, human errors, biases, judgment and choice options,

55

and learning. These characteristics can be modeled using prescriptive models, and when appropriate, can be used to enable the DSS to facilitate the decision process for the user.

There is a consensus among cognitive scientists that to demonstrate intelligent behavior, a cognitive agent needs to be able to integrate information from several sources, usually from both the agent's memory and the environment. This behavior can be enhanced with the use of an appropriately designed computer system to support the user. Although it has been said that "Knowledge is power," it is more likely that the truism actually is "Knowledge, and the ability to properly apply it, is power." Certainly in our information age this is true. The ultimate purpose of a DSS should be to provide the appropriate assistance in maximizing the user's knowledge and decision-making abilities.

All the knowledge in the world is not of much use if the person or organization possessing it does not understand how to use it properly, or even how to properly recognize it. However, with an appropriately designed computer-based support system, the decision-making abilities (including the ability to identify and use relevant information) of any decision maker are improved—in some cases, greatly improved.

## USER THINKING STYLES

The models for describing the way people think are called *user thinking styles* or *cognitive styles*. An objective of a DSS should be to assist users in their search and evaluation of data as well as the definition and resolution of issues as defined or recognized by the user. An understanding of user styles is basic to providing support. The different cognitive styles can be divided into two categories: information gathering (preceptive and receptive) and information evaluation (systematic and intuitive) (McKeeney & Keen, 1974). The descriptions of each style are

1. *Information gathering* relates to the processes by which the mind organizes the diffuse sound, sight, smell, touch, and taste stimuli it encounters, rejecting some of the information, and summarizing and categorizing the rest. Information gathering can be described on a continuum from preceptive to receptive.
   a) *Preceptive thinkers* bring to bear concepts to filter the data and focus on relationships between items and look for deviations from, or conformities with, their expectations. Precepts (i.e., data categories or trends) act as cues for cataloging the data they find. Often preceptive thinkers will ignore relevant information detail.
   b) *Receptive thinkers* are more sensitive to the stimulus itself. They focus on detail and try to derive the attributes of the information from direct examination of it. Receptive thinkers may fail to shape information into a coherent whole.

2. *Information evaluation* refers to the problem-solving process. Information evaluation can be described on a continuum from systematic to intuitive.

   a) *Systematic thinkers* tend to approach an issue by structuring it in terms of some method that will lead to a solution. However, for certain tasks they can develop a method of procedure that utilizes all their experience and economizes on effort.

   b) *Intuitive thinkers* tend to use more solution testing and trial-and-error methods. They may jump from one method to another, discard information, and be sensitive to cues that they may not be able to identify verbally. They are better able to approach ill-structured problems, in which a large volume of data, the solution criteria, and the nature of the problem prohibit any predetermined method.

One of the primary purposes of gathering data is in support of the issue detection and definition process. However, in some cases the user may need additional data for formulating or refining alternative solutions.

Most modern theories of the decision process emphasize "rationality," such as mathematical decision theory and game theory. A model of cognitive style focuses on problem solving, but decision making is above all *situational* and must include problem finding and defining. The decision maker scans the environment and organizes what is perceived. The effort is geared to both clarifying one's values and intents as well as dealing with predefined problems.

Decision makers become aware of a problem or issue in many different ways. Some problems are thrust upon them by extreme circumstances such as a company president suddenly confronted with the fact that a competitor is greatly expanding its work force. However the problem is conceived, the decision maker will often also declare his desired level for involvement in dealing with the issue.

The decision maker's involvement is limited by the formal constraints of his position (e.g., a large corporation president usually does not have the time to perform detailed analyses) and the informal traditions and expectations implicit in his role. Thus, decision making is strongly influenced by the decision maker's perception of the relevant duties of his position. A decision situation exists when some event or cue in the environment is detected and triggers an activity to begin a search-detect-define-resolve sequence that may result in a decision of some kind. The sequence is caused by, and results from, the decision maker's relationship to his pertinent environment.

Some analysts say that the focus on problem finding requires particular modes of cognition and that some of these modes are better suited to certain contexts than others. Turning this around, this implies that a given decision maker's cognitive style for information gathering and information evaluation should be considered in determining the information required for making a decision in a particular context or environment. The various cognitive styles and examples of each in a two-dimensional gathering-evaluation continuum are shown in Figure 4.1.

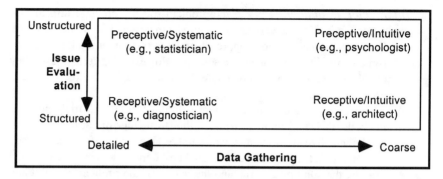

**FIGURE 4.1.   The cognitive style process continuum.**

In describing how the different personalities think, McKeeney and Keen (1974) say that

*Receptive thinkers tend to*

- suspend judgment and avoid preconceptions,
- be attentive to detail and to the exact attributes of data, and
- insist on a complete examination of a data set before deriving conclusions.

Receptive thinkers are usually better at tasks that require detailed information, such as planning or performing research.

*Preceptive thinkers tend to*

- look for cues in a data set,
- focus on relationships, and
- jump from one section of a data set to another, building a set of explanatory precepts.

Preceptive thinkers are usually better at searching for relevant data for defining an issue or for comparing the alternative solutions to an issue.

*Systematic thinkers tend to*

- look for a method and make a plan for solving a problem,
- be very conscious of the approach,
- define the quality of a solution largely in terms of the method,
- define the specific constraints of the problem early in the process,
- discard alternatives quickly,
- move through a process of increasing refinement of analysis,
- conduct an ordered search for additional information, and
- complete any discrete step in any analysis that they begin.

Systematic thinkers are usually better at resolving issues that require a structured approach, such as evaluating the various attributes of a set of alternative solutions to an issue.

*Intuitive thinkers tend to*

- keep the overall problem continuously in mind,
- redefine the problem frequently as they proceed,
- rely on unverbalized cues, even hunches,
- define a solution in terms of fit,
- consider a number of alternatives and options simultaneously,
- jump from one step in analysis or search to another and back again, and
- explore and abandon alternatives very quickly.

Intuitive thinkers are usually better at dealing with tasks or problems that require creativity, such as invention or the search for relevant data when an issue is not yet defined.

McKeeney and Keen have developed a classification for tasks and problems in general with two general categories, namely, known and unknown, for both information acquisition and information manipulation. Information acquisition is the process of data gathering, and information manipulation is the process of issue definition and resolution. From Table 4.1 it is evident that a known/known (planning) case involves a situation in which the decision maker knows both what data are relevant and what mental operations and analyses are required to deal with the data. The unknown/known (intelligence-search) case results when the decision maker understands the required operations and methods for processing the data but the data required are not known. The known/unknown case (invention) involves understood data but the decision maker does not know how to evaluate the data. The unknown/unknown (research) case exists when both the information and operations are unknown. A typical research problem in business and government will require the development of new products or new approaches to novel situations.

The user decision styles shown earlier in Figure 4.1 are linked to types of problems in Table 4.1 (where data gathering = information acquisition and issue

**TABLE 4.1.**
**Classification of Tasks and Problems**

| Information acquisition (perceptual process) | Information evaluation (conceptual process) | |
|---|---|---|
| | Known | Unknown |
| Known | Planning | Invention |
| Unknown | Intelligence-Search | Research |

"Known" means that the process is understood. "Unknown" means that the process is not well understood.

evaluation = information manipulation). Receptive thinkers like to focus on the details of the issue. They are able to gather data needed to refine the definition of an issue or to provide the data for quantifying the attributes of the alternative solutions to an issue so that they can be culled or rank-ordered. The receptive model is used to discover the relevant data for creating a better issue definition or determining the "best" issue solution.

Preceptive thinkers tend to look at the problem in a holistic sense, that is, they search for data that pertain to the entire problem, not some aspect of it. The preceptive model is used to discover how data elements might relate to one another or how data can be used to develop an initial or early definition of the problem.

The objective of the systematic thinker is to structure the problem so as to reduce the unknowns and to explicitly define all of the constraints of the problem. Using this structure, a model is developed for evaluating alternatives which can be improved with usage. The systematic model is used to understand the analytic process. The systematic thinker validates the model formally and methodically by testing it relative to known inputs and outputs. The systematic thinker has faith in the plan and the structured process.

The intuitive thinker focuses on, and enjoys playing with, the unknowns until the necessary steps for completion are found. Then the problem is often delegated to some individual who can systematically complete the solution. The intuitive model is used to discover the significant problem parameters for making useful predictions. The intuitive thinker will validate the model by experiment and test it against experiential knowledge, concepts, and expectations, placing much less faith in authority.

By understanding user styles and embedding this information in the DSS, the DSS can be used to assist the user in gathering information as well as evaluating the information. The DSS design should also consider that two or more users may be sequentially involved in the process over the entire decision process.

One method that can be used for determining user style is to have the DSS ask a few questions for which the answers will infer the user's affinity for a particular type of data gathering or data analysis. For example, the DSS could pose the following questions to the user:

Do you like to focus on details? Yes No
Do you like to examine the raw data for issue attributes? Yes No

If the answers to both questions are "Yes," then the DSS can assist the user in attempting to see the whole issue, and not just the details. Or the DSS can recognize the manner in which the specific user gathers data and will present these to the user without requests or interruptions of the user's thought processes.

The data-collection and problem-solving thinking styles described in Tables 4.2 and 4.3, respectively, are summarized in Table 4.4.

## TABLE 4.2.
## Description of Approaches for Data-Collection Thinking Styles

| Type of thinker | Cognitive approach | Characteristics |
|---|---|---|
| Receptive (data collection) | • is sensitive to stimuli (i.e., data) | • will glean much about the issue from input data, but may not see the whole picture |
| | • focuses on details, specifics, and hard realistic facts | • usually needs assistance to see the whole picture |
| | • derives attributes of data from direct examination of data | |
| | • is pragmatic in the sense that he notices "what is" rather than "what might be" | |
| Preceptive (data collection) | • likes to filter data | • is good at seeing the whole picture, but may miss important details |
| | • focuses on whole problem and relationships | |
| | • gleans information from imagination | • usually needs assistance to take note of certain details that may have been overlooked |
| | • looks for deviations or conformities relative to expectations | |
| | • has user doctrines to act as cues for defining data requirements and cataloging data | |
| | • conjectures about "what might be" as opposed to "what is" | |

## TABLE 4.3.
## Description of Approaches for Problem-Solution Thinking Styles

| Type of thinker | Cognitive approach | Characteristics |
|---|---|---|
| Systematic (problem solution) | • likes structured approaches in terms of some method that will likely lead to a solution | • is good at solving well-structured problems but is not so good at solving ill-structured[b] problems |
| | • uses impersonal, formal, or theoretical models of reasoning | • usually needs additional assistance when solving ill-structured problems |
| | • likes to generalize | |
| | • is logical and scientific | |
| Intuitive (problem solution) | • avoids commitment to particular methods | • is good at solving ill-structured[b] problems but is not so good at solving well-structured[a] problems |
| | • performs solution testing | • usually needs additional assistance when solving well-structured problems |
| | • uses trial and error methods | |

*continues*

## TABLE 4.3.   continued

| Type of thinker | Cognitive approach | Characteristics |
|---|---|---|
| | • likes to particularize<br>• is willing to jump from method to method and discards data frequently<br>• is sensitive to inexplicable cues<br>• is sensitive to people and individual differences<br>• focuses on judgments of good-bad, ethical-unethical, pleasing-displeasing | |

Notes:   [a]usually characterized by high volume of data and ill-defined criteria
         [b]usually characterized by low volume of data and well-defined criteria

## TABLE 4.4.
### Summary of Combined Data-Collection/Problem-Solving Thinking Styles

| Type of thinker | Tends to: |
|---|---|
| Preceptive-Systematic | • be conceptual and theoretical<br>• focus on concepts |
| Preceptive-Intuitive | • be humanistic, conceptual, and general<br>• focus on social and cultural ideas |
| Receptive-Systematic | • be analytic and scientific<br>• focus on technical ideas |
| Receptive-Intuitive | • be humanistic but particularistic<br>• focus on plight and concerns of individuals |

Most people are not one of the pure types of thinker; they are usually some combination of two or more of these. But they will likely be predominantly one of the four pure styles. The objective of the DSS should be to assist the user in finding the proper approach to information gathering or evaluation and then provide the needed assistance in implementing the discovered proper approach.

## EXPERIENTIAL LEVEL MODEL

Since all users do not have the same amount of experience with the organizational environment, a DSS should be designed to accommodate users of differing experiential levels. Rasmussen's cognitive control modes of novice, competent, and expert (Rasmussen, 1980) generally correspond to the concepts for cognitive styles (Sage,

1981) based on the continuum from systematic (*novice*) to intuitive (*expert*), with *competent* representing an intermediate style. These three levels or modes of cognitive control are described as follows:

- The novice user is someone who does not have experience with the particular situation that is under consideration. This means that the user may rely on methods that allow the user to break down the issue into parts that can be analyzed and evaluated separately. These methods are the structured evaluation rules.
- Competent users have some experience, but are still not experts with the particular situation under consideration. They may rely on methods that allow for elimination of alternatives, namely the comparison methods.
- The user who is an expert with the particular situation (i.e., similar situations) may not rely on the computer for assistance, being familiar with the situation under consideration and able to react with a familiar response. The expert user will rely on his judgment abilities, even when using the computer for support.

All of these users may wish to use the computer for implementing the selected response.

## DECISION STRESS MODEL

Decisions makers are often affected by stress conditions, such as fear in all its manifestations. Fear can appear as decision avoidance, feeling of pressure due to time limitations or importance of the issue, concern about the attitude of a superior toward the decision, or lack of confidence due to limited experience with the issue category.

Janis and Mann (1977) developed a decision stress descriptive model to prescribe the appropriate decision process in response to the various levels of user time-stress. It implies the type of situation assessment required for a decision maker at the various levels of conflict defined in the theory. A variation of this theory is shown in Figure 4.2. The DSS can recognize the manner in which this specific user gathers or evaluates data and may present these methods to the user without user requests or interruptions of the user's thought processes. The context of the Janis-Mann model is a single individual who is faced with typical decision situations. However, in an organizational environment, decision makers may be faced with multiple decisions, some near simultaneous, often creating a crisis environment. These types of situations are similar to the "garbage can" environment (Cohen, Olsen, & March, 1972) where time-stress can cause organizational decision makers to use limited rational approaches. For this reason, time-stress is probably paramount in defining the user's stress level, except possibly in very high risk situations.

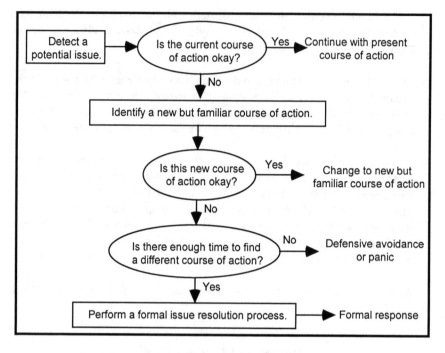

**FIGURE 4.2.   Janis-Mann decision-stress theory model.**

An important use of this model for DSS support is to assist the user in such tasks as

- gathering information that can indicate the improper continuation of the current course of action, or proper or improper change to a familiar course of action; and
- understanding defensive avoidance and panic situations through enhanced awareness of stress situations and the suggestion of a limited-rational decision strategy alternative to enable the user to quickly resolve a high stress situation.

## HUMAN BIASES

People have a variety of biases. The effects of hindsight bias and overconfidence on failures as well as successes in judgment have been studied by Fischhoff (1982) in his review of several studies; he offers a framework for debiasing. Six characterizations of the domain of biases in which recurrent patterns might be sought are

1.   the underlying processes about which inferences are required are probabilistic,

2. problems arise in the integration rather than the discovery of evidence,
3. any existing biases are nonsubstantive (i.e., no deliberate deception),
4. some normative theory is available characterizing appropriate judgment,
5. no computational aids are offered or allowed, and
6. no obvious inducements for suboptimal behavior are apparent.

In making a normative judgment on the basis of a model, there is a general principle that inductive reasoning must be justified in terms of the applicability of the underlying models of the events in question (Nesbitt, Fong, Krantz, & Jepson, 1982). Faulty perceptions of a situation can lead to misdirected reactions. There are six common ways in which experts may overlook or misjudge a situation (Slovic, Fischhoff, & Lichtenstein, 1982):

1. failure to consider the ways in which human errors can affect technological systems,
2. overconfidence in current scientific knowledge,
3. failure to appreciate how technological systems function as a whole,
4. slowness in detecting chronic, cumulative effects,
5. failure to anticipate human response to safety measures, and
6. failure to anticipate "common-mode failures" which simultaneously afflict systems that are designed to be independent.

An example of Item 6 is the failure of the McDonnell-Douglas DC-10 jet airplane control system, which consisted of three "independent redundant systems" but which all failed in the event of a structural failure, such as a rear engine explosion—which is what happened.

Four common bias errors are

1. *Pride*: the inability to see one's limitations in either data gathering or resolution determination. (Sources of this type of error are arrogance or stubbornness.)
2. *Representativeness*: the degree that object or event A is representative of the class X of objects, or events. (Sources of this type of error are: insensitivity to prior probability of outcomes, insensitivity to sample size, misconceptions of chance, insensitivity to predictability, the illusion of validity, and misconceptions of regression.)
3. *Availability*: the ease with which instances or occurrences can be brought to mind. (Sources of this type of error are: biases due to the retrievability of instances, biases due to the effectiveness of a search set, biases of imagination, and illusory correlation.)
4. *Anchoring and adjustment*: making estimates starting from an initial value that is adjusted to yield the final answer. (Sources of this type of error are: insufficient adjustment, biases in the evaluation of conjunctive and disjunctive events, and anchoring in the assessment of subjective probability distributions.)

Biases can be alleviated through the use of prompts from the DSS. For example, efforts to mitigate or de-bias data can be performed as follows:

- Make a serious attempt to perform a self-evaluation concerning decision-making abilities in all areas of the decision process.
- Encourage decision makers to distinguish between good and bad decisions associated with good and bad outcomes to avoid various forms of selective perception such as the illusion of control. Have decision makers study structured processes for decision making to learn how to use a proper decision process.
- Sample data from a broad set of sources or databases and be especially careful to include data that might contain disconfirming information.
- Avoid the hindsight bias by providing access to data from critical past times.
- Encourage effective learning from experience by attempting to understand the decision process and implementing a learning rule.
- Collect both qualitative and quantitative data. Do not overweight any of the data in accordance with personal views, beliefs, or previous findings.
- Represent data in several orderings so that data recency and primacy order effects are minimized.
- Use a structured approach to decision making based on logical processes to avoid confusing facts and values with wishful thinking.

## INDIVIDUAL JUDGMENT AND CHOICE ASSESSMENT

To make a decision, the decision maker uses decision rules, either consciously or unconsciously. These decision rules can be divided into three areas: judgment, comparison elimination, and systematic evaluation. Decision rules allow the user to intuitively cull (i.e., eliminate) and rank-order options by systematically decomposing and evaluating the formulated responses so as to identify the preferred option. Each of these choice rules is explained in more detail in Appendix A.

### Judgment Rules

Judgment rules are the methods that people use that are based on experience. They consist of standard operating procedures, intuitive affect, and reasoning by analogy. These holistic rules allow the user to select the preferred alternative based on an examination of the situation and concomitant options as a whole and go with their "gut feeling."

> *Standard Operating Procedures.* These are experienced-based guidelines for decision making which are typically used without resorting to any fundamental rationale that originally led to the procedures.

*Intuitive Affect.* Valuation is usually based on an attempt to determine whether alternatives are pleasant or unpleasant, likeable or unlikeable, or good or bad for the decision maker or his organization.

*Reasoning by Analogy.* Reasoning by analogy is accomplished by making a selection from among alternatives based on the use of analogies, prototypes, or other models which have been developed from experiences that allow a person to feel familiar with the situation.

## Comparison Rules

Comparison rules are methods that can be classified as screening or elimination rules. There are three types of comparison rules: comparison against a standard, comparison across attributes, and comparison within attributes.

## Structured Evaluation Rules

Structured evaluation rules are methods that depend on a set of well-defined steps. There are four types of systematic rules: expected utility theory, subjective expected utility theory, multiattribute utility theory, and subjective multiattribute utility theory. These rules are frequently referred to as "normative rules." Evaluation rules allow the decision maker to rank-order alternative actions so that the preferred or "best" one can be recognized. The most popular systematic rule is multiattribute utility analysis. There are variations of this rule, which depend on the manner in which the attributes relate to one another. However, the use of a linear evaluation method, even when the proper mathematical considerations are not followed, will result in an improvement over expert evaluations that are made without any assistance (Dawes, 1979).

The user can select the solution response he wants by making a judgmental decision to select the desired alternative, cull out alternatives using comparison rules (down to a single alternative if desired), or rank-order alternatives and select the highest ranked alternative.

## A LEARNING MODEL

At the end of the decision process the user may take the time, if it is available, to evaluate the process to assure that the various tasks were performed properly and comprehensively. This can be accomplished by asking appropriate questions and performing a sensitivity analysis. In essence, the user must question the decision process and examine its capability to provide the desired and needed support. If there are any errors in the process, the user should detect, identify or define, and appropriately correct them. The process by which this is done is explained below and relates to Figure 4.3.

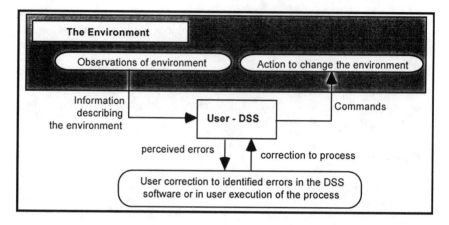

FIGURE 4.3.    The dialectical learning process.

When users are allowed to modify the DSS process without recourse to others, then the process is said to be *private* or *personal*. When the user must get permissions (usually from a designated group) to make changes, then the DSS process is said to be *public* (to the designated group) or *nonpersonal*. A properly designed DSS security mechanism will provide the appropriate protection to the DSS process so that it can be modified only by an appropriate person and circumstance.

A most efficient learning process is based on Argyris's (1982) individual and organizational learning model. This prescriptive model involves the questioning of currently implemented decision theories in an effort to detect, define, and resolve errors in these theories, as implemented in the DSS. This learning process is called double-loop learning and corrects slips and mistakes by repeating some task or procedure, or it may involve changing the currently implemented decision process as shown in Figure 4.3.

The learning process, called dialectical learning (Sage, 1990), can occur as a result of two categories of error in the decision process:

1.  errors detected during the decision process, and
2.  errors detected using feedback information after either the issue definition or the resolution implementation has been completed.

Failures in execution or unintentional actions (*slips*) and selection of inadequate approaches so that the desired outcome is not achieved (*mistakes*) require that the issue definition and resolution process be repeated from some earlier point. Slips can sometimes be detected by the DSS when a user command violates domain functional model constraints (i.e., laws of nature); then the DGMS would display one of the following messages: "Are you sure that you wish to implement the current command?" or "This command is not physically possible." In unusual circumstances, an expert user might actually wish to implement such a command, but most often the command will represent a slip.

By adhering to the Motif standards (Open Systems Foundation, 1993) for graphical interface design concepts, the human interface will be amenable to upgrades and modifications to improve the interface to accommodate desired improvements.

Many errors do require modifying the DSS to improve its support capability. Should the user feel that support requirements are not being met, based on feedback, then changes to the human interface system or other aspects of the DSS must be implemented. These causes of error are

1. changes to a familiar environment that make it different from before,
2. changes to an unfamiliar environment,
3. occurrence of an unfamiliar situation that requires an update of templates and models,
4. changes in the organization's standard operating procedures,
5. changes in the organization's goals, and
6. changes in the user's support requirements.

An objective of incorporating a user-friendly learning model into the DSS design concept is to enable users to improve both their decision-making abilities and the support capabilities of the DSS itself.

## IMPLEMENTATION OF BEHAVIORAL MODELS

There is a possibility that the DSS, with the user's assistance, can identify and define a personal profile of the user to enable the DSS to understand the needs of the user and provide appropriate assistance. The DSS can

1. determine the user-style, then recommend alternatives for data gathering or data evaluation;
2. determine the user's stress level, then recommend an issue definition and resolution strategy;
3. minimize human error and assist in recovering from errors through interface design options; and
4. allow for learning based on experience with the DSS, the issues addressed, and the relevant environment.

## SUMMARY

The alternative approaches for dealing with human behavior relevant to a DSS were described using models for user thinking styles, experiential levels, decision-stress levels, human biases, individual judgment and choice, and learning. The different user styles were presented and discussed, implying the potential for the DSS to sometimes predict the desired reasoning strategy, data gathering strategy, and issue resolution method to ensure a more user-friendly DSS. Models of biases can also be used to assist the user in identifying and reacting to human foibles by the decision maker.

# 5

## Example of a Decision Support Capability

### OVERVIEW OF THE DEMONSTRATION SYSTEM

This chapter contains a presentation of a particular decision process revealing how a decision process can be supported by a computer-based system. The decision support system used is a throwaway prototype developed using HyperCard 2.2 running on a Macintosh personal computer. HyperCard is a multimedia toolkit that can be used to create prototypes. It is based on an object-oriented-like scripting language called HyperTalk that allows a user to perform actions on the following objects: buttons, fields, cards, and stacks (Apple Computer, 1993). How an object responds to a particular message, from inside or outside the HyperCard program, is dependent on how the user has programmed the object's script. It is the object's script that is responsible for the different actions that give a prototype the capabilities it needs to emulate the desired system, in this case a decision support system. The prototype developed and presented here is called *DSS-Demo*. The software system will be explained as we proceed through the decision process as it unfolds. *DSS-Demo* was created using the concepts explained in the earlier chapters of this book.

A principle objective of the design of the *DSS Demo* is that the system provide the capability to support a user who is unfamiliar with the DSS but who understands how a personal computer operates. With user-friendly icons, suggestion buttons, and help buttons, users can get the support they need without referring to the tome that is usually provided with a software package. As the user becomes more proficient with the DSS, the design allows for the user to take short cuts to get the

71

desired support with a minimum of time and energy. Another objective of the design is to enable the user to enjoy the computer-supported process by making the DSS game-like in its operation so that decision making is exciting, productive, and enjoyable, but foremost, easy to use.

A simplified version of a common commercial issue is used to illustrate the decision theories and processes discussed earlier. The problem is the case of a company (Widgets-R-Us) that has a good market share but is losing out to a creative competitor (Widget Busters) that has introduced a lower-cost product and is gaining in market share. How should Widgets-R-Us respond? The illustrations are simple and can be easily followed by those who are intuitive as well as those who are technical, or anywhere in between.

The first few times using the DSS may be a little difficult, but as the user gains experience, his confidence will increase and the DSS will become much easier to use. This walk-through of a sample problem can be used for guidance in using this or a similar DSS.

## THE ISSUE

The relevant environment is that for a particular product, called widgets, two companies dominate the market: Widgets-R-Us and Widget Busters. Widgets-R-Us has 50% of the market and Widget Busters has 30%, with multiple companies sharing the other 20%. However, Widget Busters has recently introduced a newer version of the widget and is now rapidly increasing its market share. It is this introduction and increasing market share that have resulted in the issue detection. The overall market for widgets is gradually increasing but the level of business in dollars for Widgets-R-Us is steady (although percentage-wise it is decreasing) whereas the level of business for Widget Busters is increasing (both dollar-wise and percentage-wise).

## USING THE DSS

The initial card for the *DSS-Demo* is the Demonstration Home Card. This card presents two buttons to the user, a *Decision Support System Demo* button and a *Quit* button (see Figure 5.1). A field with a description of what the system does is also presented to the user.

## COMPUTER-SUPPORTED ISSUE DEFINITION

Clicking on the *Decision Support System Demo* button sends the user to the next card, the Main Screen that is shown in Figure 5.2. This card has eight buttons. The three principle buttons can be used to 1) define the issue (*Issue Definition* button),

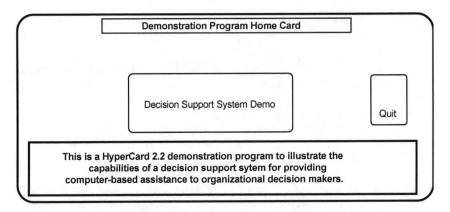

**FIGURE 5.1.** The demonstration home card.

2) resolve the issue (*Issue Resolution* button), or 3) implement the resolution (*Implement Resolution* button). The other five buttons can be used to 1) seek help (*Help* button), 2) return to the Home card shown in Figure 5.1 (*Return* button), 3) present the user's personal profile (*Profile* button), 4) explain where the user is relative to the main screen (*Where?* button), or 5) return to the Main screen, which

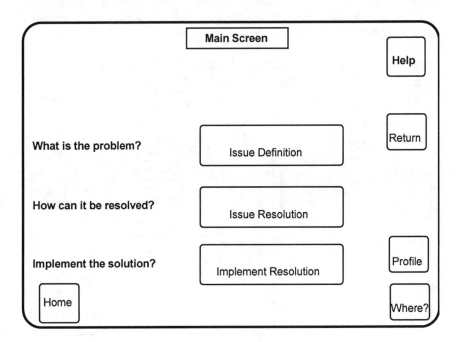

**FIGURE 5.2.** The main screen.

can be recalled at any time on any screen (*Home* button). The first four buttons are always on the right whenever they appear. The *Home* button is always in the lower left-hand corner.

If the user is interested in getting some help, then clicking on the *Help* button will yield the following message:

> When stating facts, use complete sentences.
> When creating the issue definition, use complete sentences.
> When the issue has been defined to the user's satisfaction, attempt to simplify the definition, and then proceed to resolving the issue.

Of course, the first objective in a typical decision process is to define the issue. This process begins by clicking on the *Issue Definition* button. The Issue Definition Process screen will appear.

**Informal Issue Definition**

The screen for the issue definition process is shown in Figure 5.3. There are five radio buttons on this screen: 1) *List Facts of Situation*, 2) *Input Initial Issue Definition*, 3) *Input Latest Issue Definition*, 4) *Satisfied with Issue Definition?*, and 5) *Need More Facts?*, and an additional rounded rectangular button *Add New Data*.

Clicking on the *List Facts of Situation* radio button will cause the computer to present the following message:

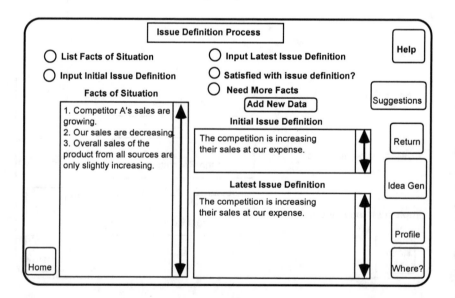

FIGURE 5.3.   The Issue Definition Process screen.

Please list the facts of the situation directly into the "Facts of Situation" field.
OK

The user should first click on the *OK* button. The initial facts will likely be information that was collected personally by the user and needs to be typed in. The initial facts are

1.   Competitor A's sales are growing.
2.   Our sales are decreasing.
3.   Overall sales of the product from all sources are only slightly increasing.

Once the facts are listed, the user should create an initial definition of the issue. This is accomplished by clicking on the *Input Initial Issue Definition* radio button. The computer will present the following message:

Please input the initial issue definition of the situation in the "Initial Issue Definition" field.
OK

Again, the user should click on the *OK* button and then proceed to create the initial issue definition based on the listed facts of the situation. The initial issue definition is: "The competition is increasing their sales at our expense." At any time, users can seek help by clicking on the *Help* button; get assistance in creating ideas needed for identifying facts by clicking on the *Idea Gen* button; get suggestions on how the issue definition process should be conducted by clicking on the *Suggestions* button; see their personality profiles by clicking on the *Profile* button; or find out where they are in the process by clicking on the *Where?* button.

For idea generation, the *Idea Gen* button will take the user to a screen[16] where the user will be asked to describe the objectives of the generation process and then to create as many alternatives as he can. These alternatives should meet the objectives of the process. Clicking on the *Idea Gen* button will take the user to the screen shown in Figure 5.4. The user should begin the session by clicking on the *List the objectives* radio button.

The computer will display the following message:

What is the objective of this creative session?
OK     Cancel

The user should type an input into the provided box. In this case the objective is: "To determine the data that are pertinent to this issue." Then click on the *OK* button. If the user is satisfied with this definition of the objective for this creative session, then the user should click on the *List the alternatives* radio button. The computer will then present the following message:

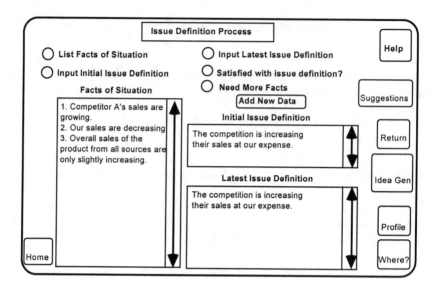

FIGURE 5.4.   The Idea Generator screen.

Please list any data elements that you think might be appropriate.
OK     Cancel

The user should respond by providing some inputs. In this case the inputs are as follows:

> market info, profits, overall business level, competitor's business level, cost to develop a new product, time to develop a new product, and risk of new product development

When the user has finished listing the alternatives, he clicks on the *OK* button. Then the computer will present the following message:

Can you think of any more alternatives?
Yes     No

If the user thinks that he can, he should click on the *Yes* button and provide additional inputs directly into the Alternatives field.

After determining the list of alternatives, the user can edit them directly on the screen—adding, modifying, and deleting the alternatives as desired in the Alternatives field.

Several screens display the *Profile* button. Clicking on this button reveals the user's personality profile in a scrolled screen, such as the profile shown below:

You are receptive to the data. You:
–are sensitive to data stimuli
–focus on details
–derive attributes of data from direct examination of data
–are pragmatic in sense that you notice "what is" rather than "what might be"
You like to use systematic approaches to resolving issues. You:
–like structured approaches
–use impersonal, formal, or theoretical models of reasoning
–like to generalize
–are logical and scientific

The DSS recommends that you collect detailed information. After you develop the initial issue definition, you should try to see the whole picture. When satisfied with the issue definition, use a structured approach to identify alternative responses and to eliminate some or evaluate them.

The profile can be used by the DSS to provide helpful hints to the user on how to proceed for data collection or for determination of an appropriate response.
Once some facts are listed and an initial issue definition has been created, the user is asked if he is satisfied with the issue definition by clicking on the *Satisfied with issue definition*? radio button, then the following message will appear:

Are you satisfied with the issue definition?
Yes    No

In some cases an Initial Issue Definition is sufficient because of time or other considerations (e.g., the issue is not very important) and the answer will be *Yes*. If not, additional data can be collected and added to the list of facts. More data can be added by clicking on the *Need More Facts*? radio button and following the directions provided by the data collection screen. When this button is punched, the screen shown in Figure 5.5 will appear.
Should the user need some assistance at this point, clicking on the *Help* button will cause the following message to appear:

–Identify any new data that might be relevant.
–Identify the potential sources of this relevant data.
–Identify the data sources that have the most credibility.
–Evaluate the data, whether the data are positive or negative.
–Add the data to the current list of relevant data items.

When the user has finished locating and describing the new data, perhaps using the Idea Generator, he then returns to the Issue Definition Process screen by clicking on the *Return* button. When the *Add New Data* button is selected, the new data will be automatically added to the list of facts.

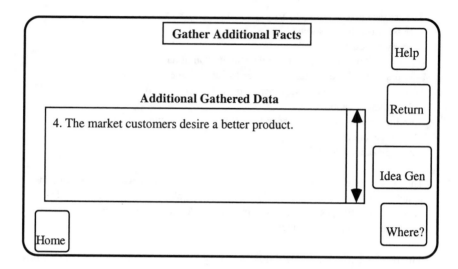

FIGURE 5.5.   The Gather Additional Facts screen.

Based on the complete list of facts and the initial issue definition, a Latest Issue Definition can be created by clicking on the *Input Latest Issue Definition* radio button, which will present the following message:

> Please input the latest issue definition directly into the "Latest Issue Definition" field.
> OK      Cancel

The user should click on the *OK* button and then type the addition to the latest issue definition in the appropriate field, "; but customers want a better product." This clause is automatically added to the initial issue definition to yield, "The competition is increasing their sales at our expense; but customers want a better product."

Complete sentences should be used to ensure that the listed facts and issues are easily understood. Using complete sentences causes the user to formulate the facts in a manner that makes the facts easier to understand. Later, when the issue definition is being formed and also when the potential responses are being formed, the facts will be easier to use as reference information. Note the examples of facts, initial issue definition, and latest issue definition as shown in Figure 5.3.

**Formal Issue Definition**

If the answer to the question *Satisfied with issue definition?* is *No*, then the user can seek additional facts or begin the process of expanding the issue definition by formally describing the issue in the field labeled Latest Issue Definition. It helps to number the facts to give some quantification to the amount of collected data. Facts and issue definitions should be terse but not so short that they are misunderstood. The original facts for this case are shown as Items 1, 2, and 3. Once an initial issue definition has been created ("The competition is increasing their sales at our expense."), the user can keep adding new data and continue to modify the issue definition as appropriate.

For the Issue Definition screen, the *Suggestions* button will offer a field that contains a description of how one might perform the issue definition process, namely:

−Develop an issue definition. Be terse for the initial definition.
−Use the facts to infer the issue definition.
−Use complete sentences when developing the issue definition.
−As more facts are accumulated, expand the definition to make it appropriate to the data and do not worry about how large the issue definition gets. Put the expanded issue definition in the Latest Issue Definition box.
−When satisfied with the final issue definition, reduce its size to make it easier to read.

If the user needs additional information, he can click on the *Need More Facts* radio button and gather additional data. When you return from this button, then click on the *Add New Data* oval button and the newly gathered data will be automatically added to the list of facts. The new data element in this case was "4. The market customers desire a better product." Using the new data element, the user can properly modify the latest issue definition to reflect the new data element, namely, adding a new clause: "The competition is increasing their sales at our expense; but customers want a better product."

If the user is satisfied with the issue definition, then he can click on the *Satisfied with issue definition?* button and select *Yes* for the answer. This will send the user back to the Main screen (Figure 5.2). At this point the user is ready to resolve the defined issue. This means clicking on the *Issue Resolution* button.

## COMPUTER-SUPPORTED ISSUE RESOLUTION

The Issue Resolution Process card or screen shown in Figure 5.6 has three principle buttons: (a) *Expert System*, (b) *Structured Processes*, and (c) *Judgment Process*. There are four radio buttons: (a) *Satisfied with issue definition?*, (b) *Satisfied with issue resolution?*, (c) *Display the Problem*, and (d) *Display the Responses*. Clicking on the *Display the Problem* button will cause the computer to display the issue in the appropriate box. Similarly, the *Display the Responses* button will cause the responses to be displayed. The DSS can be designed so that the identified problem is automatically displayed; however, in this case the user has the option to either display the problem or not. The conditions shown in Figure 5.6 display when the *Display the Problem* button has been clicked.

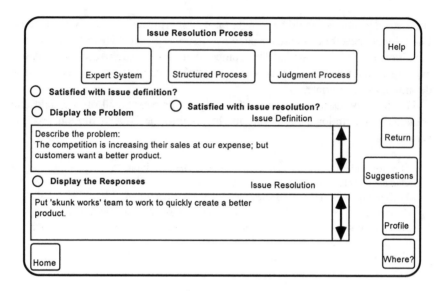

**FIGURE 5.6.   The Issue Resolution screen.**

At any time, the user can assess the issue definition or the issue resolution with the option to rework either, if that is required. Sometimes a clear understanding of the issue does not occur until the decision maker is well into the resolution process. Whenever this occurs, the user should return to the issue definition process and ensure that an appropriate issue definition is determined before attempting to find a response.

If at any time during the situation resolution process the user decides that the issue definition is not accurate, then he can click on the *Satisfied with issue definition?* radio button and then click on the *No* button. The computer will automatically proceed back to the Issue Definition Process screen so that the user can change the issue definition as desired.

### Expert Subsystem

If the user is satisfied with the issue definition, then he should click on the *Yes* button and select from among the three issue resolution buttons, the first being the *Expert System* button.

The *expert system* is for users (often domain novices) who do not understand how to resolve this issue. However, some users who understand how to resolve the issue may wish to see what the expert system says or to offload some of their responsibilities. *Structured processes* are for those who wish to eliminate some identified options or to rank-order the options to ascertain the user's preferred response. The elimination process will require using a comparison rule. The rank-ordering process will require quantifying each alternative and selecting the one with the largest numerical value as the preferred option. The *judgment process* is for those users who already possess a fundamental understanding of the issue and can define a resolution based on an analogy with a similar issue with which they are familiar.

The expert system usually consists of the organization's Standard Operating Procedures (SOPs) or some expert rules as elicited from some single expert or group of experts. These rules are in an "If X, then Y" form. That is, "If the situation is $X = x_1, x_2, \ldots$, then resolve with solution Y."

The SOPs are a set of rules that have been devised by the organization to serve as guidance for decision makers. Most of the typical problems encountered by organizational decision makers will usually be found in the SOPs. Experienced managers and others who have been in the organization for several years will usually have memorized or learned the SOPs, or at least those procedures that are considered to be the most important to their jobs.

The SOPs could be installed as a list to be viewed by the user who might be looking for assistance in making a decision in some particular area. However, when the SOPs are provided as an expert system, the user can very quickly get an organizationally appropriate response to a particular situation.

For issues that do not require creativity and which are addressed by the SOPs, use of the SOPs/expert system is an ideal approach. However, for issues that require creativity and ingenuity, even if they may be addressed in the SOPs, many users will prefer to resolve the issue using their skills. But even in these cases, the user will often wish to see what the expert system says, for at least two reasons: 1) acquiring a starting point in identifying alternative responses or 2) comparing his solution with the organizationally approved response.

In this DSS, there are multiple expert systems, and, after the user clicks on the button, the computer will request the user to identify the proper expert system. For this DSS, the following four expert systems have been named: 1) commercial (see Appendix B), 2) new business, 3) strategic, and 4) tactical.

Use of the expert system is called the Novice User Approach, that is, it is for use by a person who is inexperienced relative to this environment in general or inexperienced relative to this particular issue.

When the *Expert System* button is punched, the computer will present the following message:

Please input the TYPE OF ISSUE (commercial, new business, strategic, tactical).
OK     Cancel

The user should, for this case, type in *commercial* and then click on the *OK* button. This will automatically trigger the Commercial Expert System. This expert system has a screen (see Figure 5.7) that consists of the following radio buttons (a) *Read Environmental Data*, (b) *Activate Expert's Rules*, and (c) *Change Knowledge Base*.

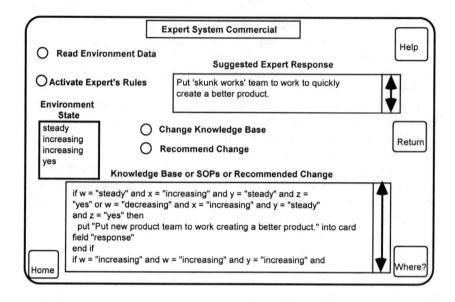

FIGURE 5.7. The Commercial Expert System.

The *Read Environmental Data* button, when selected, requests that the user provide a description of the relevant environment, which begins a sequence of message displays, with the first being

Please input our sales level (decreasing, steady, or increasing).
OK     Cancel

Type in *steady* and click the *OK* button. The next message will then appear:

Please input competitor's sales level (decreasing, steady, or increasing).
OK     Cancel

Type in *increasing* and click the *OK* button. The next message will then appear:

Please input overall sales level (decreasing, steady, or increasing).
OK     Cancel

Type in *increasing* and click the *OK* button. The next message will then appear:

Please input whether consumers want a better product (Yes or No).
OK     Cancel

Type in *Yes* and click the *OK* button.

If a response is misspelled, then the computer will state so and the user is asked to repeat the input process for this particular item. If the user clicks on the *Cancel* button, then the DSS will repeat the process for this step only.

At this point the expert system will display the four values for the current environment state in column form: "steady, increasing, increasing, Yes" (see Figure 5.7). If this is the correct description of the environment, then the user should punch the *Activate Expert's Rules* button. This description of the environment will cause the expert system to respond with the following issue resolution: "Put 'skunk works' team to work to quickly create a better product," which is placed in the field Suggested Expert Response. If the user is satisfied with this response, he can punch the *Return* button and return to the Issue Resolution Process screen described in the next section.

If the description of the environment is not correct, then the user should click the *Read Environment Data* radio button and repeat the input process described above.

If the user feels that the expert system has a problem that needs to be resolved (learning), then he can make a modification to it by selecting the *Change Knowledge Base* radio button and making the appropriate changes. The user is cautioned here to perform this action only when he is very proficient at using the HyperTalk (or other appropriate) programming language. Whenever any changes are made to the knowledge base (i.e., the expert system rules), the changes should be verified and validated through rigorous testing. If the user is not qualified to make changes to the knowledge base, or any other aspect of the Expert Subsystem, then the user should record the recommended change by clicking on the *Recommend Change* button. This button will cause the following to be displayed:

Would you like to enter a recommended change into the "Recommend Change" field?
Yes    No

The user can click on the *Yes* button and the computer will then display the following message:

Make the recommendation.
OK

The user can click on the *OK* button and proceed to type in the recommended change directly in the Recommend Change field, which will appear on the screen. The recommended change would be in the form of "The rule for the case of the environment of a, b, c, d should return the following response xxxxxxxxx." If this is satisfactory, then the user should click on the *Return* button.

At the end of the session when the response is implemented, the recommended change to the expert system will be automatically sent to the programming department with an appropriate header that describes who sent the recommended change, when it was sent, and any other pertinent information needed by the programming department.

In many cases, the client may wish to expand the screen area for the Environment State field so that a description of the environment can be provided when the situation is more complex.

If the user is satisfied with the response generated by the expert system, then the response can be implemented by the DSS. First, he should return to the Main screen by clicking on the *Return* button.

### Implement the Preferred Response

Upon returning to the Main screen (Figure 5.2), and once the user has formulated a satisfactory response to the identified issue, he can automatically implement the resolution by clicking on the *Implement Resolution* button. For a further discussion of this activity, see the end of this chapter.

### Using Personal Judgment for Issue Resolution

The user could have chosen to use any of the other methods of resolving the issue, given that they had the proper expertise. For example, if the user were proficient in the domain and had seen similar issues before, then he could have used his expert judgment. The judgment process is activated by clicking on the *Judgment Process* button, which will cause the computer to display the following message:

> Please type in your preferred response directly into field "Issue Resolution."
> OK      Cancel

Then type in the desired response and click on the *OK* button. Unless the *Judgment Process* button is punched, the user will be unable to type a response in the Issue Resolution field since the field is protected with a Lock Text on typing.

Experts are people who have many years' experience in the relevant domain and who usually know the organization's standard operating procedures. They could have seen an analogy with other issues that they had resolved before and just typed in their preferred response into the field Issue Resolution (Figure 5.6), such as: "Put a 'skunk works' team on this problem and have them quickly create a competitive product."

This method is called the Expert User Approach.

### Using a Structured Process Approach

The user could also have chosen to use a structured approach by clicking on the *Structured Process* button in Figure 5.6. This would have resulted in the Structured Processes screen shown in Figure 5.8. This screen has three primary radio buttons:

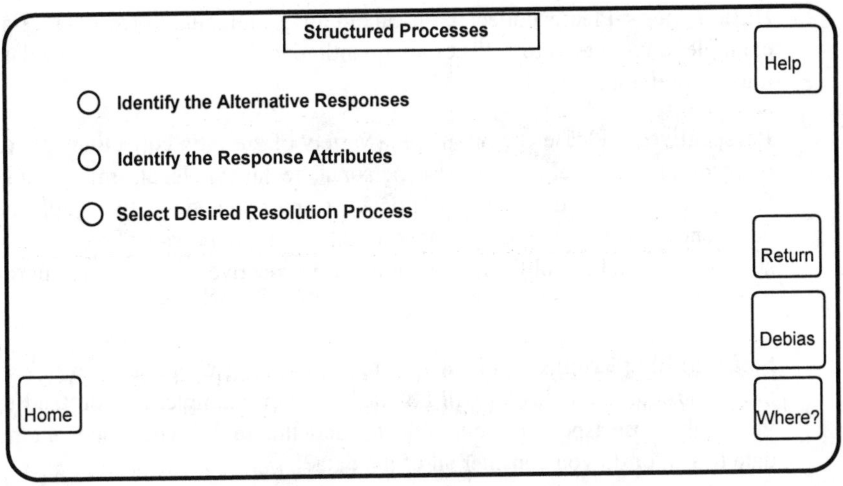

**FIGURE 5.8.  Structured processes.**

(a) *Identify the Alternative Responses*, (b) *Identify the Response Attributes*, and (c) *Select Desired Resolution Process*.

Many screens display the *Debias* button. If the *Debias* button is punched, then a scrolled field with the following information for debiasing the data or alternatives is listed (i.e., prescriptions for avoiding human foibles that affect some users) (Sage, 1981):

**Pride**—Please make sure that you examine and rectify your personal limitations in either data gathering or resolution determination. (For example, do you tend to acquire data only from sources with which you are familiar?)

**Objectivity**—Please make sure that you also seek data that might be negative towards your issue definition or your alternative responses. (For example, do you tend to seek only data that will confirm your beliefs?)

**Availability**—Please make sure that you do not just gather data that are easy to get, also consider gathering data that may be more difficult to get. (For example, do you tend to gather data from the same sources for all your issues, even when these sources may not be appropriate?)

**Sampling**—Please gather data from a variety of sources or databases. (For example, do you tend to gather a limited amount of data that may be inconclusive?)

**Weighting**—Please do not overweight any of the data in accordance with personal views, beliefs, or previous findings. (For example, do you tend to give greater credence to data that agree with your beliefs?)

**Data Types**—Please collect both quantitative and qualitative data. (For example, do you tend to collect only quantitative data when qualitative data may be preferable, or vice versa?)

**Perspectives**—Please attempt to get a variety of views in collecting data or in forming issue definitions. Use personal, technical, legal, engineering, financial or economic, design, political, or any other views that might be pertinent. (For example, do you tend to take a single perspective of issues, such as technical or political, when another perspective may be more appropriate?)

**Self-Fulfilling Prophecy**—Please try to avoid interpreting data or events so that a particular conclusion will be reached. (For example, do you tend to view only those aspects of your collected data that reveal what you want the data to say, or do you consider all of the data?)

The first task here is to identify the alternative responses by clicking on the top radio button, *Identify the Alternative Responses*. This causes the screen shown in Figure 5.9 to appear. Ordinarily the user will want to have the issue definition shown; this is accomplished by clicking on the radio button *Display the Problem*. This method is for users who wish to eliminate responses (comparison rules), rank-order the responses (systematic rules), or both.

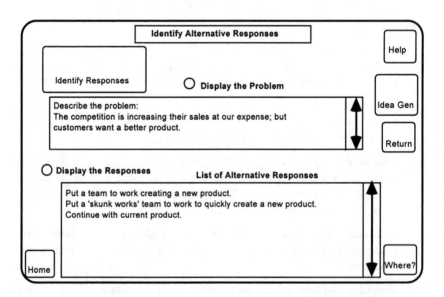

**FIGURE 5.9.   The Identify Alternative Responses screen.**

*Identification of Alternative Responses.* It is very useful to see the issue definition when attempting to identify the responses to the issue. This can be accomplished by clicking on the *Display the Problem* radio button. When developing these responses it is best to express them using complete sentences. This will help to ensure that the alternatives are stated in a form that makes them more easily understood. The identification of alternatives for issue resolution means using the issue definition and attempting to conceive of a variety of responses that could mitigate or resolve the issue. The user may wish to employ an idea generator for developing options. This can be done by clicking on the *Idea Gen* button. However, the user will likely be able to identify alternative responses by just examining the issue definition and attempting to think of how this issue might be resolved. The user can begin this process by clicking on the *Identify Responses* button. The computer will present the following message:

Please create a response to this issue.
OK     Cancel

Then type in a response, "Put a team to work creating a new product" and then click on the *OK* button. This means using a team that is made up of knowledgeable employees who can bring a new product through the life cycle process in a reasonable time.
The computer then asks,

Can you think of any additional responses?
Yes     No

Click on the *Yes* button. The computer responds with,

Please create a response to this issue.
OK     Cancel

Doing this twice more, two more alternatives can be identified: "Put a 'skunk works' team to work to quickly create a new product" and "Continue with current product." A skunk works team is a special team that can put together a high-quality product in minimal time. This team is not used unless the need for developing a new product is considered critical. The last option, to continue with the current product, essentially means to take no new actions and to hope for the best.
When the *No* button is clicked in response to the question of any additional responses, the process goes back to the Structured Processes screen, Figure 5.8. The objective now is to decide which of the response options is the best. This can be done by finding a set of parameters that can be used to quantify the "goodness" of each alternative. These parameters are called "attributes." They are the characteristics of each alternative's performance capabilities. When a satisfactory set of

responses has been identified, the user can click on the *Return* button and go back to the Structured Processes screen. To identify the attributes, click on the *Identify the Response Attributes* radio button, which will cause the screen shown in Figure 5.10 to appear.

*Identification of Response Attributes.* Any alternative response option can be rated in several different ways. For example, some attributes of an option are: purchase price, speed, risk, time to obtain, time to implement, probability of success, miles per gallon, comfort, reliability, availability, maintenance required, size, weight, beauty, operational cost, and robustness. These attributes can be rated quantitatively (i.e., using numerical values) or qualitatively (i.e., using verbal descriptions). If the attribute rating is qualitative, such as a rating of poor, fair, average, good, or excellent, then these in turn can be quantified, such as poor = 1, fair = 3, average = 5, and so forth, although they do not have to be. The attribute ratings are used to evaluate the goodness of each option.

Clicking on *Display the Responses* radio button will cause a presentation of the identified responses. Clicking on the *Identify Attributes* radio button (in the middle of the screen, Figure 5.10) will begin the process of identifying the response attributes. The computer will ask,

Do you know of an attribute?
Yes    No

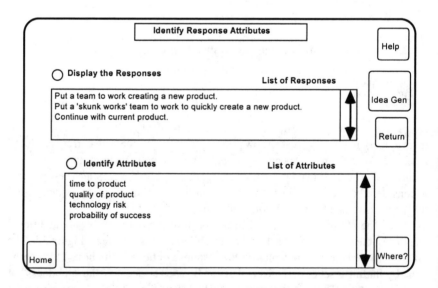

**FIGURE 5.10.   The Find Response Attributes screen.**

and the user responds by typing in the attribute and clicking on the *Yes* button. This display will be repeated until the user clicks on the *No* button.

Do this until the desired set of attributes has been listed. When all the attributes have been identified, just respond to the question shown above by clicking on the *No* button.

For this case, the attributes listed are the following items: time to product, quality of product, technology risk, and probability of success. "Time to product" means the time required to carry the new product through its complete life cycle from conception to manufacturing. The other attributes are self-explanatory.

Now, when the *Return* button is selected, the system will return to the Structured Processes screen (Figure 5.8) with the pointer designating the *Select Desired Resolution Process* radio button. Clicking on this button causes the computer to ask,

Do you wish to eliminate alternatives or to rank-order them?
Eliminate     Rank Order

Clicking on the *Eliminate* button causes the Comparison Rules screen to appear as shown in Figure 5.11.

*Comparison Rules*. This screen has four radio buttons: (a) *Comparison Against a Standard*, (b) *Comparison Across Attributes*, (c) *Comparison Within Attributes*,

**Comparison Rules**

Help

○ Comparison Against a Standard

○ Comparison Across Attributes

○ Comparison Within Attributes

○ Judgmental Comparison

Return

Debias

Home

Where?

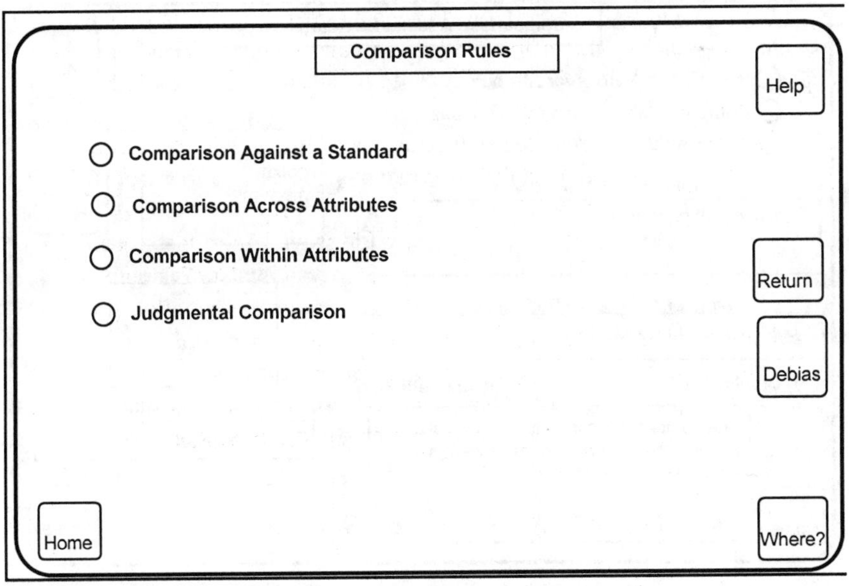

**FIGURE 5.11.** The Comparison Rules screen.

and (d) *Judgmental Comparison*. See Appendix A for explanations of these (Sage, 1981). Clicking on the *Comparison Against a Standard* button causes the screen shown in Figure 5.12 to appear.

The Comparison Against a Standard screen (Figure 5.12) has three major radio buttons: (a) *Identify St[andar]d. Values for Attributes*, (b) *Comp[are] Att[ribute] Val[ue]s vs St[andar]ds (All must pass)*, and (c) *Comp[are] Att[ribute] Val[ue]s vs St[andar]ds (One must pass)*. Clicking on *Identify Std. Values for Attributes* causes the computer to request "Please input the standard for this attribute." The computer will automatically request four values since it knows there are four attributes for this case. Respond by typing in *100* for this standard. This means it should take 100 days to begin manufacturing a new product using this option. The computer will ask,

> Is bigger better?
> Yes    No

The answer is *No*, since the longer it takes to produce the product the worse it is for the business. The computer will then state,

> Please input the minimum value for this attribute.
> OK    Cancel

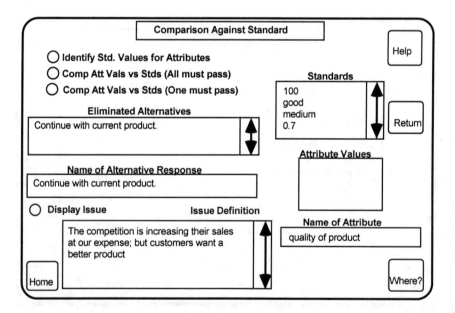

FIGURE 5.12. The Comparison Against a Standard screen.

The response is *0*; punch *OK*. The computer will then state,

Please input the maximum value for this attribute.
OK    Cancel

The response is *150* and *OK*.

Similarly, for the other attributes the standards are *good*, *medium*, and *0.7*. *Good* means that the quality of the product is acceptable. For the second attribute, *good*, bigger is better, and the minimum is *fair* and the maximum is *excellent*. *Medium* means that the technological risk is acceptable. For the third attribute, *medium*, bigger is not better, and the minimum is *low* and the maximum is *high*. And for the last attribute, *0.7*, bigger is better, and the minimum is *0.0* and the maximum is *1.0*. Thus the standard values for this case are *100* [days], *good*, *medium*, and *0.7*, respectively, for: time to product, quality of product, technology risk, and probability of success.

Now there is an option of performing a *conjunctive* comparison (all attribute values for each alternative must be at least as good as the standard) or a *disjunctive* comparison (at least one of the attribute values for each alternative must be as good as the standard), or else the alternative is eliminated. For this case choose *Comp Att Vals vs Stds (All must pass)*. This causes the computer to respond "Please input the value for attribute 1." The user types in *100* and clicks on *OK*. Similarly, the computer will ask for the other three values which are *good*, *low*, *0.7*. For the next alternative, the values are *50*, *excellent*, *low*, *0.9*. For the last alternative, the values are *0*, *fair*—this causes the computer to state "This attribute value fails the conjunctive standards test." and the user should click on *OK*. This will cause the computer to place the alternative "Continue with current product" into the Eliminated Alternatives field, to delete the last alternative from the list of response options, and to diminish the number of alternatives by one.

Since we are through at this point with the comparison rule, clicking on the *Return* button sends the system back to the Comparison Rules screen (Figure 5.11), clicking on the *Return* button sends the computer back to the Structured Processes screen (Figure 5.8), and clicking on the *Return* button sends the system back to the Issue Resolution Process screen (Figure 5.6). At this screen the user can click on the *Satisfied with the resolution?* button and respond with a click on the *No* button.

Since there are two alternatives remaining, the user will wish to rank-order the remaining alternatives. Return to the Structured Processes screen and click on the *Select Desired Resolution Process* radio button and pick the *Rank Order* process option. This will take the user to the screen shown in Figure 5.13.

*Structured Evaluation of Alternatives.* Systematic rules are methods that depend on a set of well-defined steps (Sage, 1981; Sage, 1990). A favorite method for rank-ordering alternatives is multiattribute utility analysis. These rules are frequently referred to as "normative rules." Evaluation rules allow the decision maker

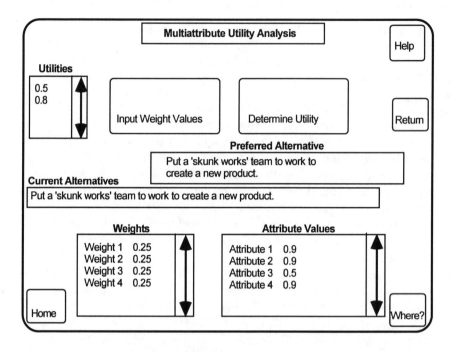

**FIGURE 5.13.    The Multiattribute Utility Analysis screen.**

to rank-order alternative actions so that the preferred or "best" one, in the opinion of the user, can be recognized.

The theories for the various systematic rules are based on rather strict assumptions and hypotheses for the implementation of a specific rule (Fishburn, 1970). However, linear rules have been shown to be better than expert judgment, even when strict interpretations of implementation have not been observed (Dawes, 1979). The identification of the attributes of the alternatives should consider that they should be "preferentially independent." That is, the attributes should be identified and selected such that the assessed value assigned to any attribute should not be affected by, nor affect, the values assigned to the other attributes. Each of these attribute values should be some number $v$ such that $0.0 \leq v \leq 1.0$.

Weights are the importance factors assigned to each attribute and should sum to one. The objective of a systematic rule is to assign a numerical value called the Utility of Option $A_i$ to each option $A_i$ such that if,

Utility of Option $A_j$ > Utility of Option $A_k$ for any j and k, then the option $A_j$ is said to be preferred to $A_k$. If the utilities are equal, then there is no preference between the two options, either option is just as acceptable as the other. If the equal value options are the most preferred, then a comparison method can be used to eliminate one of them.

At this point the relevant alternative options and the response attributes have been identified. The systematic process begins with the user clicking on the *Input Weight Values* button. The computer then presents the following message:

Please input the value for the first weight.
OK    Cancel

If the user wants equal weights, he should type in a "1" for each weight and punch the *OK* button. Otherwise, he can type in the desired weight and punch *OK*. The system knows the correct number of weights needed. If the weights do not sum to one as they should, the DSS will state "The weights do not sum to 1.0, will normalize" and will normalize the weights so that they sum to one. The user can view the displayed weights and decide if the weights are satisfactory. If they are not, just repeat the process by clicking on the *Input Weight Values* button and proceed as before. For this case, equal weights of 0.25 were used. This implies that the different attributes have equal worth or meaningfulness.

When the weights are satisfactory, click on the *Determine Utility* button. The DSS will display the first alternative and present the following message:

Please input the value for the first attribute.
OK    Cancel

Respond by typing in *0.5* for the "time to product" value and click on the *OK* button. The computer will then state "Please input the value for the next attribute." Respond with 0.5 and click the *OK* button. The next two attributes are similarly *0.5*. After the four attribute values are provided by the user, the computer will automatically display the overall utility, which is 0.5, and go to the next alternative, the skunk works alternative. The computer will state "Please input the value for the first attribute." Respond with a *0.9* input. The other attribute values for this alternative will be *0.9, 0.5*, and *0.9*.

The computer will reveal the utility for this alternative, 0.8, and put this alternative in the Preferred Alternative field, namely, "Put a 'skunk works' team to work to quickly create a new product." The user should then click on the *Return* button, which will take the user back to the Main screen.

The utilities for both the normal team and the skunk works team options are displayed, 0.5 and 0.8, respectively. The computer will automatically select the better of these two options and display the preferred one in the Preferred Alternative field.

The last part of the decision process is then to implement the preferred resolution by clicking on the *Implement Resolution* button, which will reveal the screen shown

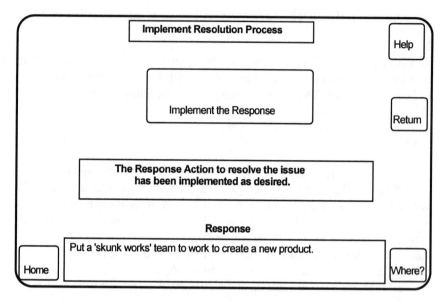

FIGURE 5.14.    The Implement the Preferred Response screen.

in Figure 5.14. Then clicking on the *Implement the Response* button will send the correct commands to the proper people within the organization. If the user desires, the computer will display the messages and addresses of those receiving the directions generated by the Implement Resolution process.

By enabling the computer to implement the resolution, the decision maker is freed to begin the process of making other decisions. This could release a considerable burden on many decision makers (Smith, 1992).

# III

## Creating a Decision Support System

# 6

## Identifying the Requirements for a DSS

### WHERE DO REQUIREMENTS COME FROM?

Before we can begin the process of creating a decision support system, we need to know what the requirements for this system are. A process for properly identifying the requirements is very important when designing and developing a DSS. The determination of system requirements means identifying the needs and desires of the client or owner organization of the system to be built. A system requirements process can be divided into two parts:

1. determining the user requirements, and
2. determining the specifications for the system.

*User requirements* are the needs, as expressed by the organizational users, for the DSS to support their decision-making activities. User requirements are gathered from the client organization either by getting the requirements statements from the user or by asking the user pertinent questions and using the answers to these questions to create the user requirements. User requirements can be confirmed and approved by building a prototype system and getting customer responses to the system. Once a set of acceptable user requirements has been developed, a set of system specifications can be identified. *Specifications* are the statements that specify the system requirements at a level from which the system architecture can be determined.

Requirements analysis is one of the most important phases in software development. "Requirements specifications are typically generated by the requirements analyst after consulting with the user" (Hsia et al., 1994). This approach of relegating users to an indirect role may be the root of some of the failures that occur in actual cases of software development. Too often very sophisticated schemes with complex computer system support are devised that seem to work in an academic or restricted setting, but which are not applicable to real world organizations, since they do not consider the organization itself and the particular circumstances.

Some organizational characteristics that should be considered in requirements engineering are shown in Table 6.1. The effects of the characteristics are included. It is likely that no specific requirements engineering methodology will work for all organizations in all circumstances (Hsia, Davis, & Kung, 1994). The structured approach explained here can properly be characterized as "brainstorming."

This chapter offers a description of the processes for requirements identification and validation. It also includes a description of how an independent verification and validation (IV&V) can be performed on the user-validated requirements. A requirements development methodology that has proven successful is presented and some observations and results of using this process are discussed. It is believed that a non-computer-supported approach that uses an organizational perspective for cer-

**TABLE 6.1.**
**Typical Organizational Characteristics and Effects**

| Organizational characteristic | Potential characteristic effects |
| --- | --- |
| Type of organizational culture | If the culture is oriented toward consensus decision making, then a group decision process is appropriate. |
| Type of mission of the organization | The user requirements should relate to the organization's mission and it is important to keep this in mind. |
| Maturity level of the organization | An "initial" or ad hoc maturity level implies that a sophisticated computer support system may not be appropriate and a more hands-on process (generally non-computer supported) may be preferred. |
| Users are nontechnical and time constrained | Taking the time (which may be extensive) to explain a sophisticated tool for requirements engineering may be prohibitive due to time constraints on the users. |
| Nonrelevant users may defer to relevant users | Because it may be well known that relevant users are knowledgeable regarding a particular business area, other users may be reluctant to comment in the relevant user's area. |
| The number of relevant users is large | It is difficult to meet with a large proportion of the relevant users who need to be directly involved in the process. |
| There is no existing requirements set | When the users are the repository of organizational functional knowledge, then users must be intimately involved in the requirements engineering process. This means that user knowledge for question responses is crucial in deriving and validating requirements. |

tain software development situations would be of interest to many requirements engineering analysts.

This chapter covers the identification of user requirements, user validation of these requirements, and the process for IV&Ving these requirements. The extent of the process presented here is limited to high-level requirements. Some pertinent definitions are included in a Glossary. Only the portion of requirements engineering that comprises identifying, validating, and independently assessing the requirements is considered in this chapter.

The methodology used here is a structured approach with pragmatic considerations concerning the users. The IV&V approach taken is also a structured approach to efficiently use limited time and personnel. The pragmatic considerations for performing requirements IV&V in this context are drawn from Sage (1992) and Sage and Palmer (1990).

## SOME ASSUMPTIONS

There are two extremes in the continuum of assumptions about requirements for information systems, perfection and inexactness, as defined below:

- **Perfection**—Requirements must be perfect and one must develop and iterate a set of requirements until they are assessed as being perfect.
- **Inexactness**—Accept that the requirements will never be perfect and hence it really doesn't matter how poor they are because they will have to be changed anyway.

Both of these extreme assumptions can lead to an untenable situation. The first because one will never achieve the condition of perfectly stated requirements. The second because if the requirements are too poorly written, the later life cycle activities will be muddled and inaccurate. Thus, the developer of requirements must take an interim position with regard to identifying requirements, accept that they will not be perfect, but also realize that the requirements must be accurate enough to assure that the architecture developed from the requirements will be satisfactory.

Even though the requirements set will never be perfect, this should not cause complacency among users, since a poorly formulated set of requirements can lead to the development of an improper architecture and thence to the selection and acquisition of inappropriate hardware and software.

One method for rectifying imperfections in the requirements is to use prototyping and an iterative process during the remaining life cycle phases. This is illustrated in Figure 6.1. This process also can be used to improve the architecture and other life cycle products. In this context of life cycle development, the role of Total Quality Management is the assurance that the products of each life cycle phase are responsive to the requirements statements.

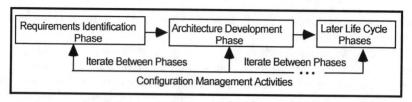

**FIGURE 6.1.   The nature of requirements improvement.**

Requirements are statements that describe the purposes of an extant or proposed system. They are based on the *purposes of the system*. Requirements should be in the form of statements that describe the functions that will achieve the stated purposes. The concern here is only with requirements. Requirements take the form of ".... shall provide .....," ".... shall ensure .....," ".... shall support .....," ".... shall display .....," ".... shall record .....," and other such actions.

Requirements or *organizational level requirements* are for specifying the system structure (i.e., the system architecture), identifying interface boundaries, and defining a list of applications or projects. System requirements or *application level requirements* are much more detailed than organizational requirements and are added later as the needs arise. System requirements define the different project needs and are used to define and develop software.

Thus, knowing what the requirements will be used for should assist the users in deciding how accurate and detailed they must be. In this phase, the requirements can be identified essentially in the following manner:

- researching through relevant documents,
- interviewing users, and
- performing analyses of the collected material.

Requirements sources are people who, or any documents that, can express what the proposed system must do. The sources of requirements can include the following:

- knowledgeable people within the organization,
- master plan documents,
- concept of operations,
- data plans,
- business area analyses,
- government agency mandates, and
- business reengineering documents.

The process of developing a set of requirements is to define the system's purposes so that they accurately infer the basic functions that need to be performed.

This description of the basic functions forms the set of requirements. One can then define a set of structures needed to perform the functions. This set of defined structures is called the "architecture."

Some basic issues for requirements include

- What constitutes a complete set of requirements?
- How good (viz., correct) must the requirements set be?
- What is the desirable level of aggregation and decomposition of the requirements set? (i.e., how detailed must the requirements be?)

Unfortunately, there seem to be no good answers to these questions that will hold in all cases. The analysts and users must decide for themselves, based on considerations of their particular situations, what the answers to these questions are. This means that performing a good requirements determination is as much an art as a science.

## USER INTERVIEWS

Requirements are dynamic, especially for large-scale complex systems, and will likely be in a state of flux throughout the entire life cycle process. Dynamic requirements mean that the critical ingredients of a requirements process are to

- develop a *baseline set of requirements* to give a starting point for later changes,
- use *configuration management* to ensure a formal process for improving the requirements set, and
- develop the requirements specifications so that they are amenable to an *architecture and system design that allows for relative ease in updating subsystems throughout the life cycle process* in response to changes in requirements and new technologies.

User requirements for an information system represent those needs that the system users desire and are generally divided into two categories (Sage & Palmer, 1990):

1. *functional requirements* that describe how a needed activity achieves a system purpose, and
2. *nonfunctional requirements* that describe a desirable or needed constraint or attribute—such as security—of the system to be built, and includes quality factor requirements, such as reliability, maintainability, and availability.

User requirements can be identified in essentially three ways:

1. market research or other studies (e.g., business process reengineering studies),

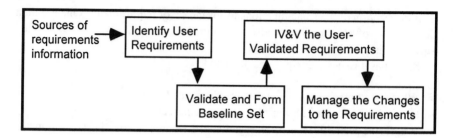

**FIGURE 6.2.**   A requirements development process.

2. users' statements (e.g., interviews with users), and
3. analyses (e.g., research of documents on mandates and directives or logical analyses).

Requirements originate from three sources:

1. customers,
2. organizational members, and
3. sometimes mandating agencies.

When mandates are levied on the organization, these mandates are essentially "constraints" on the requirements, not requirements themselves. A requirements development process is shown in Figure 6.2. Whether security and privacy are requirements themselves or limitations on how data are handled is debatable. The mandates can be treated either as requirements or as constraints. However, the reader should note that security and privacy affect who has access to data and how data are handled, so that the effects of security and privacy are limitations on system functions and other aspects of security and privacy functions unto themselves. For example, how data should be accessed to ensure privacy is a constraint of database access privileges, whereas how a user logs onto the information system is a sequence of well-defined actions or functions.

## VERIFYING AND VALIDATING REQUIREMENTS

User requirements are statements based on the *purposes of the system.* Informal user requirements are in the form of nontechnical statements which describe the functions that will achieve the stated purposes. User requirements or *organizational level requirements* are for specifying the overall system structure, identifying boundaries, and defining a list of applications or projects. Software system requirements or *application level requirements* are much more detailed than user requirements and are added later as the needs arise.

An approach could be to identify three levels of user requirements by determining

1. a *high-level set* of general requirements (organizational level requirements primarily for inferring the system architecture),
2. a *medium-level set* of more detailed requirements (interim level requirements for inferring the system interface requirements), and
3. a *low-level set* of very detailed requirements (application level requirements for inferring the software system requirements).

A more detailed requirements process can be described as follows:

1. identify an initial set of prebaseline requirements;
2. meet with a group of relevant users to review the prebaseline subset and consensually approve, amend, add, or delete specific requirements;
3. during these group decision process meetings, scribes should take notes on the issues and changes;
4. document these intermediate requirements and issues;
5. if there is an unresolved issue, then have later meetings with the users to review the issues;
6. at the later meetings, the issues from the earlier meetings and any others that the users had discovered in the hiatus should be discussed and appropriate actions taken; and
7. then assemble the final user-validated requirements for documentation as the *baseline set of high-level or organizational requirements.*

The necessary level of detail of the requirements usually cannot be determined objectively. Since the early set of requirements is ostensibly for use by the architects, the needed level of detail can be fairly coarse. Whatever the requirements turn out to be, they should be capable of defining the organization's DSS infrastructure, which comprises the hardware, software, telecommunications, people, management processes, and organizations that make up the organization's decision-making system.

Unlike the requirements for a jet plane, for which one knows equations and constraints for the system and does not need to ask a cross-section of pilots what they want the plane to be capable of doing (Heninger, 1980), determining an organization's decision support system requirements requires asking the users what they want the proposed system to do. Identification of the prebaseline requirements also may include reviewing relevant documents and responding to mandates.

The requirements set should "characterize the desired system," that is, it should accurately imply the following eight needs:

1. the user interfaces needed,
2. data that must be used, transmitted, and stored;
3. business processes to be performed;
4. information processing functions to support the business processes;
5. telecommunications systems and their quality in terms of reliability, maintainability, and availability, and general capability and timeliness;
6. security and privacy levels;
7. human resource considerations; and
8. organizational responsibilities.

This list is meant to be exhaustive, but not in priority order, because priorities are subjective and are probably context- and organization-dependent.

Validation of the initial set of requirements also requires participation by the users. The organization's domain may be large and complex and there may exist no models or equations to explain the process functions. The knowledge of the system generally resides in the minds of the users. In essence, the users represent a multidisciplinary group that understands what the organization does and hopefully what it should do during future operations. Thus, an approach to this "wicked" or ill-structured problem (Radford, 1990) is to validate the requirements with no computer assistance in a group setting, relying heavily on the knowledge of the users.

For this case, an organizational or societal perspective is required. A validation process is shown in Figure 6.3. This process is based on having identified a strawman set of requirements that needs to be validated.

The characteristics of these validation meetings, as depicted in Figure 6.3, might be described as follows:

1. a facilitator from the organization runs the group process meeting;
2. a representative from the requirements contractor explains the validation process and presents the prebaseline requirements to the group;
3. meetings start at or near a specified time;
4. discussions are allowed to go on indefinitely, but if a discussion of an issue appears to be nonproductive or divergent, the discussion is steered back to the main issue by the facilitator or an attendee;
5. only knowledgeable users relevant to a specified subset of the requirements to be discussed are invited;
6. if some organization invitee does not show up, then either a specified replacement should be assigned to attend, or the invitee should review the relevant requirements subset in private and either phone in his comments or relay them through a specified replacement;
7. if some organizational people leave early, then a designated replacement should be assigned to take over their duties at the meeting; otherwise the requirements review process will suffer;

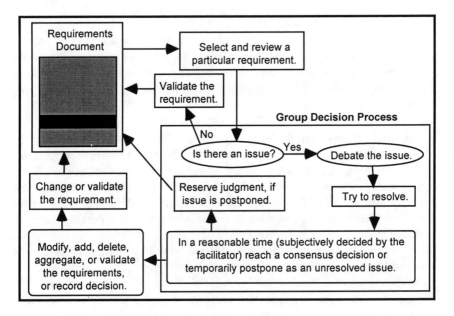

**FIGURE 6.3.** A requirements validation process.

8. the requirements contractor should provide a scribe to record all relevant statements, especially changes to the requirements;

9. the requirements contractor should update the requirements per the statements made by the participants;

10. the requirements contractor should record any issues that are raised during the meeting;

11. the requirements contractor should mail the recorded issues to all participants after the meeting for their review prior to any later meetings to resolve the issue; and

12. during the later meetings, all earlier unresolved issues and any issues identified by attendees during the period since the last meeting should be reviewed and adjudicated.

It is critical to the success of the requirements effort that the top management in an organization be fully behind the requirements process. When this is true, then lower-level management and other users will be directed to fully cooperate.

The organizational culture or perspective implies a requirements validation approach with the following characteristics (deduced from Table 6.1):

1. a group setting,

2. a unique set of ad hoc procedures appropriate for the organizational culture,

3.  non-computer-supported,
4.  selected organizational users are invited to the validation meetings,
5.  the group meetings should be categorized according to the types of requirements being considered at a particular meeting; and
6.  the requirements should be formulated essentially from scratch, mostly relying on interviews with users.

An informal approach can be used because a formal process takes away the validation process from the users who are the best qualified persons to perform this job. That is, a conversational language should be used to express the requirements. Unfortunately, unlike mathematics, the terms used in requirements engineering are not rigorously identified and defined. Thus, a concomitant glossary is necessary for the formulated requirements process used in this effort. A proposed glossary is included at the end of this chapter.

A pragmatic approach to assessing requirements is to set deadlines for the assessment process and assist the users in consensus agreement on the issues raised. In validating the requirements, the organizational users are more capable of adjudicating the completeness and correctness of the requirements than anyone else.

A large part of assessing completeness is identifying what wasn't there but should have been. Correctness is similar in that assessing correctness requires knowledge of what is functionally appropriate. Only those users who are very familiar with the relevant domain have this knowledge.

The requirements must be good enough so that system architects can accurately specify an architecture and project managers can appropriately define relevant business processes. The objective is to identify a set of requirements that is "incompleteness tolerant." There is no theory on what constitutes an incompleteness-tolerant set of requirements. The assumption here is that when the users accept the requirements statements, then that constitutes validation. So the ultimate measure of successful completion of the requirements process is the extent of user satisfaction with the requirements. After user-validation of the requirements, a requirements IV&V process should be performed.

**Configuration Management**

A process of managing changes, often called Configuration Management (CM), is the process for controlling changes to the design as they occur. Given a set of identified requirements, for each requirements statement

1.  identify each issue (i.e., detect a problem with some requirement);
2.  formulate, analyze, and interpret (i.e., define) the issue;
3.  define alternative solutions to the defined issue (i.e., restate the requirement);
4.  analyze and evaluate effects (e.g., effects on other requirements) of alternatives and eliminate poor choices;

5. select the preferred alternative;
6. implement the preferred solution;
7. test the solution; and
8. verify and validate the solution.

Configuration management of the requirements is a continual and never-ending process that will continue indefinitely throughout the life cycle phases of the information system upgrade program. It is a fact of life that the decision support system requirements will be imperfect in many ways, no matter how they are developed. The organization cannot define them and then freeze them, since new needs or imperfections are continually discovered. So what can the organization do about it?

One aspect of a solution is that the architecture can be designed for migrating from the legacy system to an open system environment (OSE). The OSE is a concept of distributed clients and servers with standard software capabilities that can enable the decision support system to be efficiently and effectively defined, designed, acquired, implemented, operated, and maintained with regard to dynamic requirements. The standards required to assure migration to an OSE must be identified, but not as part of the high-level requirements identification process.

An open environment is a system with subsystems, hardware and software that are interoperable, portable, and scalable. Interoperable means that the subsystems will easily communicate with one another. Portable means that hardware or software may be easily moved from one node to another and will easily operate at the new site. Scalable means that a subsystem's capability can be easily increased or decreased. More formally, the definitions of these are

- **Interoperable**—The effective interconnection of two or more different computer subsystems (applications, databases, or network hardware) in order to support distributed computing and/or the exchange of data.
- **Portable**—A portable computer subsystem can be moved from one node in the system to another with little or no change.
- **Scalable**—A system is scalable if it can be made to have more (or less) computational power by configuring it with a larger (or smaller) number of processors, amount of memory, interconnection bandwidth, input/output bandwidth, and amount of storage, without interrupting service.

## Independent Verification and Validation (IV&V)

Verification is a test to see if the requirements are realistic. Validation, on the other hand, is a test to see if the requirements as stated are what the users intended to say. Thus, verification is concerned with getting the requirements right and validation is concerned with getting the right requirements.

Experience with IV&V has revealed that traceability of information system upgrade requirements is a very complex and labor intensive effort (i.e., if done with no computer supporting tool), at least partly due to the number and size of the reference documents involved. However, unless the documents have been generated with appropriate formats for both reading in hard copy form and for facilitated reviewing in electronic form, then the computer-supported process becomes more difficult. Until a computer tool is acquired or developed, the tracing of the requirements will be a difficult task.

However, other aspects of the IV&V assessment can be performed. The IV&V results can be recorded as a finding (the issue) and recommendation (the resolution) format. Some of the results might be (Smith, Morgan, & Wilson, 1994)

1. there is a need for using process models for supplementing the requirements identification process,
2. the structure of the requirements document does not allow for ease in locating a specific requirement for review,
3. there is an inconsistent use of terms,
4. some of the requirements are unclear,
5. some terms are unnecessary or redundant,
6. some requirements overlap with other requirements,
7. there is a preliminary decomposition of some requirements, and
8. a few requirements implied in the business reengineering studies have been inadvertently omitted from the requirements list.

Each of these above findings, with a suggested remedy, could be briefly explained as follows:

1. **Models**—If process models had been developed, then the requirements might have been more easily identified. Furthermore, when decomposing the high-level requirements, the models will assist in identifying the more detailed requirements. This can be resolved by including the development of process models.
2. **Document Format**—It is important to format the requirements document so that a particular category of requirements can easily be located. This is particularly true when the document is in electronic form. This can be resolved by appropriately improving the document format so that the requirements can be easily located using a simple computer algorithm.
3. **Terms**—Many of the terms used in the requirements statements were not used in a consistent manner. Usually, this was caused by the lack of a thorough glossary. This can be resolved by including additional terms in the glossary.
4. **Unclear**—Some of the requirements were not stated in a manner that enabled a clear and unambiguous interpretation. This can be remedied by restating particular requirements.

5. **Redundancy**—Some requirements had terms or phrases that were redundant. This can be resolved by restating the requirements using defined terms that were added to the glossary.

6. **Overlap**—Some of the requirements statements overlapped with other requirements statements. This can be resolved by restating the affected requirements.

7. **Preliminary Decomposition**—Some of the requirements were decomposed into several high-level requirements when they should have been aggregated as a single requirement. This can be resolved by deleting (for the high-level case) the decomposed requirements.

8. **Inconsistent Attributes**—Some of the parent requirements (in the hierarchy of requirements) did not have as complete a set of attributes as some of their children had. This can be remedied by identifying a more appropriate attributes set.

9. **Omissions**—Although the requirements had been derived, in part, from the business reengineering studies, in some cases, some of the implied requirements were omitted. This can be mitigated by including a few additional requirements.

## PUTTING REQUIREMENTS INTO EVERYDAY WORDS

Based on observations of the group meetings and analyses of the user-validated requirements, some comments on the process might be as follows:

- Even though the requirements are often heavily debated, many problems will remain. Without having an unending debate on every requirement, there will likely be unidentified issues. A principal purpose of the IV&V analysis is to find and resolve these issues.

- There is a tendency among some users to identify requirements for the way things are done now, not how they should be done based on business process reengineering studies for the target system. This can be remedied by having a meeting facilitator who can detect such an incident and prompt the audience appropriately.

- The process of building models of the organizational processes or functions will facilitate the requirements identification process. It also will make the process more complex, for some, and take longer. However, when identifying requirements for a large and very expensive system, what should be considered an excessive time? For the later decomposition analyses, the use of process models will facilitate the identification of the more detailed requirements needed for defining the software system or application level requirements.

- The business process reengineering studies are quite involved and in some cases it is possible to inadvertently omit some of the implied recommendations from the studies. This perhaps can be remedied by having the reengineering study personnel include an exhaustive list of recommended requirements based on their study analysis and results. Another remedy would be to require that users be thoroughly familiar with the business process reengineering studies prior to attending the meetings to discuss the requirements.

- An objective of the organization is to improve its maturity level with regard to the Software Engineering Institute's software engineering levels by moving from an *Initial organization* (Level one), which is characterized by the use of ad hoc procedures, to a *Repeatable organization* (Level two), which is characterized by the use of structured procedures to be followed in a rule-based environment (Paulk, Weber, Garcia, Chrissis, & Bush, 1993; Paulk, Curtis, Chrissis, & Weber, 1993). This migration can be facilitated by creating, documenting, and using structured processes for formulating, analyzing, evaluating, and resolving issues, in a more formal manner.

## CREATING AN ARCHITECTURE THAT MEETS REQUIREMENTS

No matter how well the client requirements statements are expressed, some client users will most likely disagree with at least one requirement. Hence, generally speaking, the client requirements will never have the full backing of all client personnel. Even if one were able to wave a magic wand and create an immediate set of requirements that were fully approved and validated by the client, then later, and as the days pass, the requirements will gradually change to new and slightly different sets as changes are incorporated to rectify the discovered imperfections. Discovered imperfections occur due to different perspectives, variations in the interpretation of organizational purposes, newly identified needs, and other issues regarding the requirements.

## A PROPOSED REQUIREMENTS ENGINEERING GLOSSARY

To facilitate the analysis and presentation of results, a glossary of definitions pertinent to requirements engineering is useful for understanding the requirements process and the results of that process. This glossary is complementary to the discussion of an approach to requirements identification and evaluation presented in the body of this chapter. This glossary is mostly based on two references (IEEE, 1984; Lindland, Sindre, & Solvberg, 1994).

**Appropriate**—The capability of a specification to capture, in a straightforward manner, what is free of implementation considerations and the concepts germane to the system's role in the environment for which it is intended (such as business data processing, process control, communications hardware, and so forth).

**Complete**—A specification is complete if

- everything that the software is supposed to do is included in the specification;
- all pages are numbered, all figures and tables are numbered, named, and referenced;
- all terms and units of measure are provided, and all reference materials are present; and
- no sections are marked "to be determined."

**Consistent**—A specification is consistent if no requirements subset is in conflict with any other subset.

**Constructable**—A set of requirements is constructable if there exists a systematic approach to formulating requirements.

**Correct**—A specification is correct if every statement represents something required of the system to be built and no error will affect design.

**Coherent**—A specification is coherent if it is logically connected and understandable by nontechnical users.

**Customers**—Customers are the people who buy the product or service.

**Descriptive statement**—A descriptive statement is a description included in the requirements set which assists in understanding the requirements, but which is not a requirement itself.

**Executable**—A set of requirements is executable if one can construct a functional simulation of the requirements before starting design or implementation.

**Expressive**—This is the capability to express everything that needs to be modeled without much effort from the modeler.

**Formal requirement**—A specification is formal if it is built in a formal language to permit a mechanical analysis of the specification.

**Functional requirement**—A functional requirement describes how a particular needed activity achieves the purpose(s) of the system to be built.

**Incompleteness tolerant**—A specification is incompleteness tolerant if errors in the specification will have little or no effect on the system architecture and design.

**Informal requirement**—A specification is informal if it is stated in nontechnical informal language, such as English, and facilitates user understanding of the requirement.

**Minimal**—A specification that does not overconstrain system design is minimal.

**Modifiable**—A requirement is modifiable if the structure and style are such that one can make any necessary changes to the specification easily, completely, and consistently.

**Nonfunctional requirement**—A nonfunctional requirement describes a desirable or needed constraint or attribute of the system to be built, and includes quality factor requirements, such as reliability.

**Precise**—A specification is precise if one can develop a procedure to determine if some realization does or does not meet some particular requirement.

**Requirement**—A requirement is a textual description of something that the system to be built must be capable of doing, and is either stated or approved by the system users.

**Specification**—A specification can be either a single requirements statement or a complete collection of requirements statements for an entire system.

**Testable**—A set of requirements is testable if there are cost-effective procedures that let one verify that the design and/or realization of some component satisfies its functional and nonfunctional requirements.

**Tool**—A tool is any structure or process that facilitates the achievement of any systemic task.

**Traceable**—A set of requirements is traceable if the origin of each requirement is clear and it is easy to reference each statement in future documentation.

**Unambiguous**—A requirement is unambiguous if it is understood by non-computer-specialists without too much effort.

**User requirements**—These are the requirements as stated by and for users.

**Users**—These are the personnel who will actually use the system to be built.

**Validated specification**—A validated specification is an assessment that all requirements statements are correct and relevant to the domain.

**Verified specification**—A verified specification is an assessment that all requirements statements are complete and consistent.

# 7

# A Decision Support System Architecture

## CREATING AN ARCHITECTURE

When most people hear the word "architecture" they immediately think of a science associated with the design of some sort of building. However, the meaning of the word architecture has come to include the more general concept for creating a design of any structured thing, including a computer system. A discussion of a computer system design can begin with the ideas associated with the design of a building.

Heyer (1966) says that buildings are often described with esthetic terms such as abstract, geometric, organic, natural, soaring, holistic, open, and continuous. For a genius architect, clients can describe their desired new home requirements using only these esthetic terms. This was the case of the Kaufmann House (known as "Fallingwater") that Frank Lloyd Wright designed and built in 1936. This abstract approach would not be appropriate for a large-scale, complex, client/server system. Many user and architect details are required. However, building architecture adages could be used, such as "form follows function," but one might also add that "function follows need."

Another analogy from the world of building architectures is the notion first published by the Roman architect Vitruvius about 2000 years ago, who recommended a holistic approach to creating an architecture (Morgan, 1914). He defined a set of parameters needed for creating a building architecture to be all those variables that were either involved in using the building (i.e., the user requirements) or those affecting the users and builders of the building (i.e., the system requirements). Similarly, today when one creates a client/server system architecture, a fundamental requirement is to identify and define those variables that will have a significant effect on the users and the system itself. Then develop the system architecture with regard to these variables.

In the case of designing a client/server system, an architecture is a description of how the clients (i.e., the users' personal computers) and the servers (i.e., the service providers of storage, database management, and network operations) should be produced. It is a guide to be used by engineers and programmers for guiding them in their efforts to create the system as desired by the users. Thus, the architecture should reflect the system requirements as expressed by the users. A client/server architecture should contain a description of how to build the client/ server system.

Current information system architectures for client/server systems are generally distributed, open-system environments where the hardware and software can be heterogeneous and subsystems are interoperable (i.e., subsystems can interface with one another), portable (i.e., applications can be placed on different computers), and scalable (i.e., subsystems can be expanded without interruption of service). The client/server model provides a logical way of organizing the network computing environment for sharing resources. An individual computer system can be thought of as a client, a server, or both. In the client/server model, a local client application requires data from a database on a remote machine, then the client software requests the server to access the database and to provide the data. The network provides the connectivity between clients and servers in a transparent manner to the user.

Organizations usually want four things from a client/server network that provides communications connectivity for a set of decision support systems (i.e., clients). The network should be

1. *open* so customers can achieve the promise of portable systems,
2. *distributed* so customers can place their data and their users wherever it makes best sense,
3. *interoperable* so customers can confidently add pertinent new technologies as they become available, and
4. *based on standards* so that customers can purchase heterogeneous software and hardware systems that offer the most desirable characteristics, such as price and performance.

Client/server computing is a processing model in which a single application is partitioned among multiple processors (front-end [client interface] and back-end [server activities]), and the processors cooperate to complete the processing as a single, unified task. A client/server bonding software product ties the processors together to provide a single-system image (illusion). Sharable resources are positioned as servers offering one or more services. Applications (requesters) are positioned as clients who access authorized services. The entire architecture is endlessly recursive, that is, servers can become clients and request services of other servers on the network, and so forth (Boar, 1993).

Many decision support system applications are provided in a client/server environment because these kinds of systems meet the needs of customers who wish to have access to large amounts of data such as that which is accessible through the Internet. The architect can achieve a robust design by using an extensible design that can be developed using a prototype of the decision support system.

**Extensible Design**

A recommended approach to creating a DSS architecture is to use an extensible design. An extensible design is one in which the client can add on additional capabilities as they are needed in order to meet the current system requirements, which are dynamic and ever-changing. This requires an approach based on the essential requirements that can be used to create a core architecture. This core architecture should be created in a manner that allows the client to easily add on other capabilities as they are needed.

A concept for an extensible architecture is shown in Figure 7.1. The extensible concept is based on identifying a set of basic or core requirements which are used to create a core element architecture. This core architecture is designed so that it can be easily extended to include other known requirements and newly derived requirements as they arise during the life of the system.

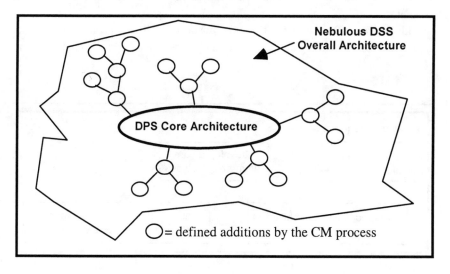

**FIGURE 7.1.** **An extensible architecture concept.**

A process for creating an extensible DSS architecture is shown in Figure 7.2, and the steps are described below.

Define a *core element* of the DPS in such a manner that this element is relatively simple and can be built rapidly and easily. The core element should be defined such that the essence of the DSS needs are fulfilled, that is, it is a basic building block. Then subsequent additions can be defined and added to eventually bring the core element up to the full desired capability.

The process is based on beginning with a roughly identified set of DSS requirements. However, the process works even if one should have very well-defined DSS requirements. Given the overall DSS requirements, select those requirements that appear to be the most important. This is likely to be a subjective process but should be as objective as possible. Use a consensual process with a group of knowledgeable designers.

A core element of a complex information system, such as a DSS, consists of the fundamental capabilities of the system as deduced from the identified user requirements as shown in Figure 7.3. Note that although the DSS requirements are dynamic, the core requirements should be reasonably static. This is the primary purpose of defining the core architecture.

The process of identifying these basic requirements is more an art than a science and depends on the developer's experience and knowledge. The developer must understand those requirements which constitute the basic needs of the DSS.

Once the core requirements have been identified, then a prototype of the core element system can be created. Test the core architecture and modify it according to the desires of the users. Add new capabilities until the overall user requirements are met.

This approach is not unlike the old Lockheed, Kelly Johnson, skunk works approach of understanding the basic needs and quickly building a system that meets

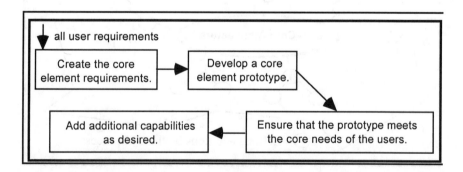

**FIGURE 7.2.   Creating an extensible architecture.**

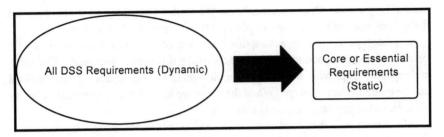

**FIGURE 7.3.    Defining the core element requirements.**

these needs. The following suggestions are recommended to assist in ensuring that the development of the software is achieved in an acceptable manner:

1. Use object-oriented programming techniques.
2. Use commercial-off-the-shelf (COTS) architectural solutions, when feasible, efficient, and effective.
3. Use a client/server architectural design.
4. Have a *general idea* of the overall concept of the DSS.
5. Have a *very good and detailed concept of the core element* of the DSS.
6. Have a *reasonably good concept of the expansion* (migration) of the core element.

Defining and building a restricted core element will keep the DSS design simple, easy-to-do, and on a short schedule. This approach has the following advantages:

1. It allows for an organization to have a clear understanding of the DSS project, technically and managerially, so that it can be properly managed.
2. It allows for an organization to develop the basic DSS element without having to understand the overall architecture.
3. It allows the developer to clearly understand what needs to be done so that he can perform efficiently and effectively.
4. It allows for a quick design, programming, testing, and implementation of the total system (hardware and software).
5. It allows for later modifications to be defined relative to the dynamic DSS requirements, rapidly changing information technologies, and better understanding of the development of the overall DSS requirements and architecture.

**Prototyping**

The primary objective of prototyping a DSS is to create a system that can be used to confirm the user requirements. An initial approach to the creation of a prototype is to develop an architecture in terms of the screens, the human-computer interface, desired by the users. Of course, the elements revealed on the screens should perform the actions needed by the users to perform their required job functions.

A prototype is usually a simplified version of the DSS that can be easily developed and provided to potential users to see if it meets their needs. The users are expected to provide feedback to the designers so that appropriate corrections can be made to the prototype. When the users are satisfied (or some time limit has been met), the prototype phase is completed.

The prototype is then used as the basic design for the operational system. There are two fundamental kinds of prototypes: throw-away and evolvable.

*Throw-Away.* A throw-away prototype is one that, when the designer is finished with it, can be discarded. The objective of a throw-away prototype is that a simple version of the DSS is developed that can be used to evaluate and correct the requirements as identified by the users. The user requirements become the objectives of the DSS prototype. Throw-away prototypes can be programmed in very user-friendly languages, such as HyperCard (Apple, 1990), ToolBook (Symetrix, 1990), or others.

Some clients think that discarding a prototype results in wasted effort. However, many developers have wasted much time attempting to evolve a throw-away prototype into a usable system when the prototype should have been discarded and an operational system developed from scratch. Some developers think that all prototypes should be called throw-away, since they will eventually be thrown away in any case.

*Evolvable.* Evolvable prototypes are used as the heart of the operational system by simply extending the prototype to include the capabilities inferred by the users. Evolvable prototypes must be developed in a language that can be used as the operational language, such as Visual Basic. Many clients prefer that prototypes be evolvable, since the feeling is that no effort is wasted. This may or may not be true. Trying to evolve a prototype that has a poor design relative to the operational needs of the users can result in much effort being expended, sometimes for a lost cause. However, with an appropriate architecture, an evolving prototype can be developed that meets the needs of the users and is economical. The designer and the client need to examine the particular situation to determine which kind of prototype is appropriate. The current sets of compilers such as Visual Basic, Power Builder, and Visual C++ offer languages that are amenable to both prototyping and evolving into an operational system. Thus throw-away prototypes appear to becoming a thing of the past.

The concepts of evolvable and extensible should not be confused. An evolvable prototype is one that can be improved to become the operational system. An extensible design for an architecture is one that can be improved to include additional or different capabilities as the system requirements are added. An extensible design allows the developer to create a simpler system that can do the fundamental activities needed by the organizational users, but can be easily modified to include new or different requirements as they are needed. An extensible design can be tested using either a throw-away or evolvable prototype.

## THE HUMAN-COMPUTER INTERFACE SYSTEM

A very important aspect of a DSS is the human-computer interface (HCI). The popular interface for today's users is the graphical user interface (GUI, pronounced goo-ey) or visual user interface (VUI, pronounced view-ey). The GUI or VUI offers direct manipulation of icons and other symbols for achieving the DSS objectives of the user. The computer interface provides the user with presentations and dialogues for enabling the user to control what the DSS is doing (Grudin, 1989; Sage & Palmer, 1990; Sprague & Carlson, 1982).

There are many possible dialogues for sequence control. These dialogues are inherently linked to the representational forms that are used for database and model base management. Among the alternative dialogues are (Smith & Mosier, 1986)

1. *question and answer and form-filling* (usually for DSS novice users);
2. *menu selection and function keys* (usually for DSS competent users);
3. *command, query, and natural languages* (usually for DSS experts); and
4. *graphic interaction* (for all types of users).

Generally, all four dialogue types should be available, since DSS users may wish to change formats as the nature of issues, and their experiential familiarity with them, changes. The dialogue generation and management system should provide various HELP facilities that support the DSS user. It should also provide navigational aids to assist users in understanding where they are in the decision process.

The DSS should support both the situation assessment process and the situation resolution process. The principal objective of any HCI is to present needed information to the user in an easy to understand manner, and to allow the user to easily input responses or commands to the computer. Often the HCI design will be specific to the user or client organization. This means that the appropriate HCI design will depend on the designer, who must acquire the interface requirements from the users or clients.

## THE DATABASE MANAGEMENT SYSTEM

The database management system (DBMS) is the software that provides for generation, manipulation, and control of the data used by the DSS. The DBMS will likely be provided by an external package such as FoxPro.

A database system is usually organized according to a data model so as to provide a framework format for the representation and manipulation of data. The three favorite data storage models have been (Eldred & Sylvester, 1994)

1. hierarchic,
2. network, and
3. relational.

All of these models are record-based, although they differ in the way they organize records. These database models were designed primarily for applications that processed large amounts of data that were relatively simple and fixed-format. DBMSs based on these models, along with sophisticated indexing and query-optimization techniques, have served business-oriented database applications especially well (Hurson, Pakzad, & Cheng, 1993).

The trend today is away from relational database management systems to object-oriented database management systems. Object-oriented databases combine object-oriented concepts, programming constructs, and database management capabilities. They support the concurrent and referential sharing of objects and alleviate the mismatch between the operational levels of database query languages and conventional programming languages (Khoshafian & Abnous, 1990).

Object-oriented systems are designed to handle complex objects dealing with data such as

1. audio,
2. video,
3. images,
4. structured documents, and
5. real-time financial feeds.

RDBMSs have difficulty in handling such objects, even with Chen's object-attribute-relational databases (Khoshafian & Abnous, 1990).

The object model is hierarchical, whereas the relational model is tabular in nature. Some say that relational databases suffer from "semantic poverty," that is, they have difficulty in establishing complex relations among different entities. For example, in an autoparts domain, an RDBMS breaks down when asked to join a large number of tables to find the parts that make up a crank shaft. An object-oriented approach would have no such problem. Fortunately, many users have data that are tabular, and RDBMSs handle these data easily and efficiently.

A comparison of the relational and object-oriented approaches to data management is shown in Table 7.1.

**Some Alternative Commercial Subsystems**

There are many alternative DBMSs currently available. Some of them are Oracle, Informix, Sybase, and FoxPro. All of these are relational database management systems. Many of these DBMSs are extending their capabilities to include object-oriented management also.

**TABLE 7.1.**
**A Comparison Between Relational and Object-Oriented Databases**

| Relational methods | Object-oriented methods |
|---|---|
| Only data are stored. | Data plus data manipulation methods are stored. |
| Data are independent. | Encapsulation and classes are independent. |
| Data can be shared and data can be accessed directly. | Data can be used only by methods of classes and data are accessed by specific methods only. |
| Data are passive. Certain limitations may be automatically triggered when the data are used. | Objects are active. Requests cause objects to execute their methods. Data and methods may be highly complex. |
| Users perceive the data as columns. | Data may have complex structures. |

## Data Warehousing and Data Mining

In a *data warehouse* solution, databases are implemented based on a business data model. They are often segmented into subject areas and may receive, reorganize, and aggregate data from operational systems in which the technology and underlying data model inhibit exploratory and analytical uses of the data. Data warehouses tend to have very large database storage capabilities and smaller versions are being developed called *data marts*.

The traditional DBMS stores and presents data in ways that optimize computer resources and data entry, whereas the warehouse presents data in terms and forms that relate to business and decision-making constructs. The primary advantage of the data warehouse method is that it offers efficient availability of relevant data to the DSS user.

One advantage of a data warehouse is the facilitation of *data mining*. Data mining is the use of business data to perform such activities as

- accurately identifying buying trends,
- optimizing promotional programs,
- precisely defining market segments, and
- determining any other parameter(s) that can be gleaned from the available data, such as analyzing customer behavior, iteratively refining criteria, setting up complex criteria for conducting searches, and aggregating complex criteria and ranges for conducting complex data searches.

## THE MODEL-BASE MANAGEMENT SYSTEM

Many DSS users do not include a data modeling capability. That is, they do not desire to have a model-base management system. System modeling is the activity of using models, usually mathematical in nature, to analyze and evaluate issues that can be modeled in an analytical manner.

The most important characteristic of model base management is that it should enable the user to explore the situation through the use of the databases by a model base of algorithmic procedures and management protocols that allow the DSS user to extract knowledge from the data in the database management system. Other desirable attributes of model base management are that it should (Dolk, 1988; Geoffrion, 1989)

1.  *provide multiple models* to accommodate user needs for flexibility;
2.  *provide an on-line capability* to access, create, modify, validate, execute, and store models; and
3.  *provide three types of bases*, personal (for access by each particular user only), semi-personal (for access by the user and selected others), and public (for access by anyone), in a group context.

Support models can be presented in the context of *means* and *ends*. The means are the processes one would use to achieve the desired ends in a decision situation. The ends are the environmental objectives that need to be achieved in some manner. Domain support models are models of the *means* for resolving the issue and the *ends* which are the goals to be achieved.

One view of models is that they can be embedded in the DSS, with the database acting as an integration and communications mechanism. From a management perspective, a model base contains routine and special statistical, financial, management science, and other quantitative models that provide the analysis capabilities in a DSS (Turban, 1990).

**Some Alternative Commercial Subsystems**

Some shrink-wrapped MBMS programs now available are the following:

- *MATLAB* is an extensible, interactive technical computing environment that seamlessly integrates computation, visualization, and modeling on PCs (The Math Works, Inc.).
- *Computer Assisted Engineering* provides automatic/adaptive boundary element refinement, relative error detection, and 3-dimensional symmetry conditions (Integrated Engineering Software, Inc.).
- *FilterCAD* contains all of the synthesis equations and numerical solutions necessary to design simple or complex, high-order, multistage filters (LinearX Systems, Inc.).
- *O-Matrix* is for integrated data analysis with a high-level matrix language, extensive graphics, functions, and a debugger (Harmonic Software, Inc.).

### Creating and Using Models

If there is a need for a modeling capability, the models can be created and used to perform analyses and evaluations, such as answering "what if?" questions.

## TRAINING VERSUS SYSTEM CAPABILITY

One of the trade-offs when creating a DSS is the desire to have a system that requires little training through a high-quality HCI versus the desire to provide lots of training so that the HCI capability may be minimal. The first approach requires a more thorough development and programming process whereas the latter requires a more thorough training effort. This trade-off should be addressed by the clients at the beginning of the DSS effort.

## CLIENT/SERVER ENVIRONMENT

Many users have a need for a client/server environment. The concept of multiple clients and servers is shown in Figure 7.4.

The concept has the following attributes (Boar, 1993):

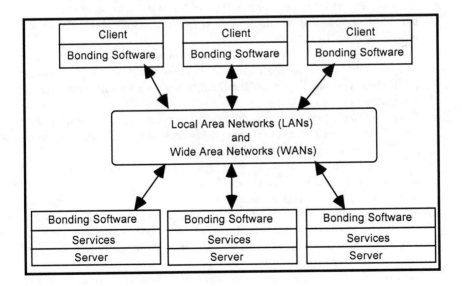

FIGURE 7.4. A client-server system.

1. Multiple clients may access multiple servers.
2. A server may provide multiple services.
3. A service may be offered by many servers.
4. The architecture is endlessly recursive, that is, servers may also act as clients and request services from other servers.
5. The client-server architecture is understood to be a "many-to-many" architecture. This distinguishes it from the "one-to-many" architecture of the traditional host-centered computing environment.
6. Local area networking and wide area networking are used to connect geographically dispersed clients and servers together.
7. A software layer called *bonding software* is located in both clients and servers, and handles the message routing between participants. Bonding software provides the illusion of a single system to the user and is commonly referred to as *middleware*.

There are seven basic actions in migrating from a legacy system to a client/server environment (Boar, 1993):

1. *Develop an information architecture* that defines the system at an abstract level.
2. *Treat data as a critical corporate resource* and assure that its definitions be put under data administration control.
3. *Develop all new software within the framework of a presentation, processing, and data layer with strict interfaces* to facilitate the later partitioning of the application into clients and servers.
4. *Treat the embedded base of databases and file systems as legacy servers* to exploit the adaptability of client-server computing to move presentation and processing away from the host.
5. *Put the decision-support database architecture in place* using extracts from the many on-line transaction processing (OLTP) and operations support systems (OSS) databases, and implement the client-server environment using business applications.
6. *Revalue the legacy systems* using the existing applications as the equal of their replacement value. The cost of redoing the business may not be as overwhelming as first anticipated because of
   - improved features/functionality through reengineering of the business,
   - changing computing economics,
   - reusability through servers, and
   - improved development productivity through modern computer-assisted software engineering (CASE) development methods. (Generally speaking, CASE tools have proved to be of little, if any, use, especially the more complex integrated alternatives.)
7. *Use proper data administration by creating OLTP and OSS subject databases as decoupled servers* that are accessed through the client-server architecture.

As distributed database management systems technology matures, create logical servers by placing these management systems on servers that are compatible (because of proper management and administration) and accessible (because of the client-server architecture).

## A PARTIAL GLOSSARY OF RELEVANT TERMS

Some client-server concepts relevant to a DSS architecture are defined below (Boar, 1993):

**Backbone Network**—A high-capacity electronic trunk connecting lower capacity networks.

**Heterogeneous System**—A distributed system is heterogeneous if it contains more than one kind of computer.

**High Performance Computer**—At any given time, high-performance computers are a class of general-purpose computers that are both faster than their commercial competitors and have sufficient central memory to store the problem sets for which they are designed. Computer memory, throughput, computational rates, and other related computer capabilities contribute to performance. In addition, performance is often dependent on details of algorithms and on data throughput requirements. Therefore, a quantitative measure of computer power in large-scale scientific processing is difficult to formulate and may change as the technology progresses.

**High-Performance Computing**—This is a type of computing that comprises advanced computing, communications, and information technologies, including scientific workstations, supercomputer systems, high-speed networks, special purpose and experimental systems, the new generation of large-scale parallel systems, and systems and applications software with all components properly integrated and linked over a high-speed network.

**Migration of an Information System**—The migration process incrementally changes from a current, unacceptable system to a client-server architecture.

# IV

## Creating a Decision Support System

# 8

# Building and Using the DSS

## REQUIREMENTS FOR THE DSS

There are three basic options usually available for a DSS customer: Buy a DSS commercial off-the-shelf (COTS) package and use it as is, buy a COTS package and modify it, or build the DSS to one's desires. For customers desiring a behaviorally oriented DSS, COTS packages that have the characteristics described in this book do not exist. An example of a behaviorally relevant DSS is described in chapter 5, but the DSS described in that chapter is only a prototype.

The requirements for the DSS can be identified as discussed in chapter 6 and depend on involving the customer or organizational users. Once the designer has satisfactorily identified the user requirements and translated these into system specifications, the DSS design process can begin.

In creating the DSS, the development of a stand-alone system will be described—that is, a system that is not connected to any other personal computer in a formal network, but which may be connected to the Internet or other database service. This system will contain the following items:

- a personal computer with a floppy disk;
- a monitor, keyboard, and mouse;
- a printer;
- a modem; and
- appropriate software.

This basic system allows a user to receive a visual or audio presentation from the computer and to input from either the mouse or keyboard to the computer. Some of the newer computer systems also allow voice input, but these systems are usually limited in their vocabulary and also may have problems understanding some of the user's verbiage. Of course the computer may receive inputs from a compact disk (if the system has one) or a floppy disk, but these are not immediate inputs from the decision maker, which is what is of interest here.

The modem allows the user to acquire data from sources such as the Internet or other electronic databases. The software should include an operating system (e.g., Macintosh 7.5.3), an Internet system (e.g., America Online), a relational database management system (e.g., FoxPro), a word processor (e.g., Microsoft Word), a spreadsheet (e.g., Excel), a compiler (e.g., Visual Basic), and a prototyping language (e.g., HyperCard 2.2).

These are the basic tools one needs to operate a personal computer system to create a DSS that can be used for typical decision-making operations. As mentioned before, the creation of a DSS design should consider that the DSS will likely be expanded to include additional capabilities as time passes.

## DESIGNING THE DSS

In creating a DSS design, the designer should consider that the DSS will likely undergo some changes to meet the dynamic needs of the customer. An example of how a design can be formulated so that it can be easily extended later is the comparison rules situation. There are four comparison rules: a) comparison against a standard, b) comparison across attributes, c) comparison within attributes, and d) judgmental comparison. These alternatives can be put on a single screen as shown earlier in Figure 5.9 and repeated here as Figure 8.1.

The designer may create an original design that only has only a single active rule, namely, comparison against a standard. However, the system should be designed for any of the four alternatives should the user wish to extend the capability later. This extensible design comes about from the engineering designer understanding the potential of the complete set of comparison rules, but the designer does not have to actually implement all of them. Each of these rules is explained in Appendix A.

## PROTOTYPING THE DSS

The development of a prototype of the DSS can begin once the designer has identified the DSS requirements and created a system design. The prototype should be an implementation of a simple version of the design with the intent of allowing the user(s) to test and evaluate the DSS screens.

For example, a developer can create a HyperCard prototype using novel screen designs that meet the user requirements but make the screens interesting and game-like to keep the user's attention to the decision process.

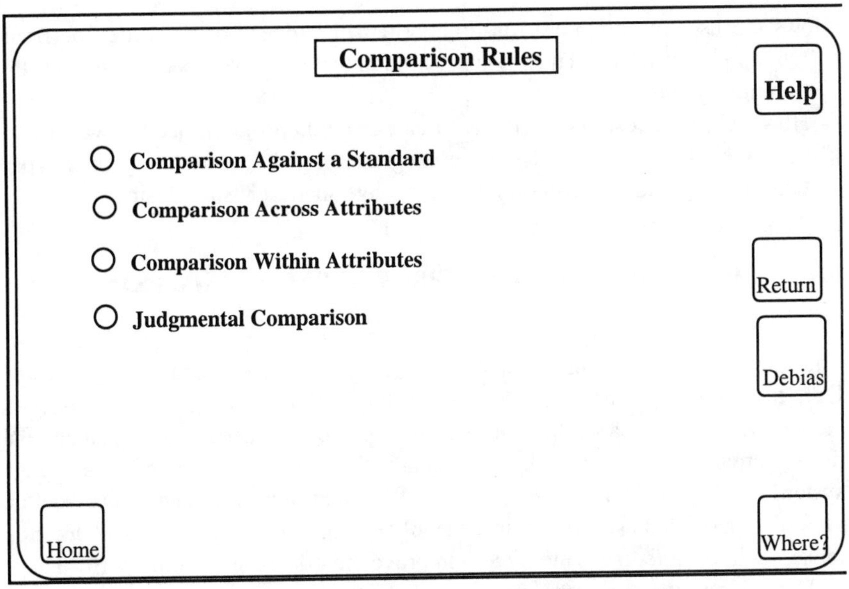

**FIGURE 8.1.    The Comparison Rules screen.**

Once a prototype process has begun, the software must be debugged. The method used here was to create a simple sample case study with known outcomes. Then, by using the case study inputs, the developer can use the prototype for processing the inputs and seeing if the prototype gives the proper answers. If not, then examine the system to identify the problem and then fix the prototype when the problem has been found. This is a typical process that programmers use to debug their software.

## TESTING AND EVALUATING THE DSS

The testing and evaluation process objective is to allow the organizational users to experiment with the DSS to see if it does what they wish it to do and to see if the DSS screens can perhaps be improved in some way. When any problems are discovered, users should note the error and describe what they would like to have the system do.

## IMPLEMENTING THE DSS

Users can actually use the prototype as the operational system if they wish. In some cases, this may mean having to load the prototype interpreter in order to run the system (such as for HyperCard), but some prototyping software, like ToolBook, allows the user to compile a run-time system that does not need the ToolBook software in order to run. Thus, it is possible to use the prototyped software as the operational system.

However, most customers will prefer an efficiently programmed software package for their DSS. This will require programming the throw-away prototyped system in an operational programming language such as Visual Basic.

## THE ADVANTAGES OF IMPROVED DECISION-MAKING CAPABILITIES

There are many advantages for an organization to distribute a behaviorally oriented DSS throughout the company. Once a behaviorally responsive DSS has been created that has the capabilities to provide the support needed for organizational decision makers, the users within the organization can acquire and begin using the system to support their decision making. With a system designed to provide the kind of support that users desire in a friendly environment, organizational decision makers will be able to use the DSS to improve their decision-making performance and hence improve the overall performance of the organization.

The DSS should be capable of providing the following:

- improved identification of relevant information,
- improved understanding of the relevant issues,
- improved definitions of relevant issues,
- improved issue resolution, and
- improved implementation of decisions.

### Improved Identification of Relevant Information

Frequently, the quality of information is dependent on the source of the information. Thus, keeping an account of the sources of information where the data quality was high is a good indicator of where to find the best data.

It is useful to keep a table that reflects information about the data sources and the data. A sample of the attributes of data is shown in Table 8.1. When the need for data in a particular area occurs, the user can perform a search of the "attributes of data acquisition" relational database and discover the costs, time, data quality, and so forth for data in that area and then select the preferred data source(s). The

**TABLE 8.1.**
**Attributes of Data Acquisition**

| Cost | Time | Area | Effort | Quality | Credibility | Source |
|------|------|------|--------|---------|-------------|--------|
| $2.00 | 5 minutes | Product description | Minimal | High | Good | Internet-Technical Information, etc. |

preferred data source(s) can be determined using one or more of the comparison or structured evaluation methods described in Appendix A. All of these methods are available to the DSS user to compare or rank-order any set of alternatives for any issue including data parameters and data sources.

Some recommended data acquisition attributes are

- cost to acquire,
- time to acquire,
- area or type of data (e.g., technical, financial, etc.)
- effort required to get the data,
- quality of the acquired data,
- credibility of the data (i.e., how believable are the data?), and
- the sources of the data.

### Improved Understanding of Relevant Issue

Because the DSS requires that the user gain a proper understanding of an issue prior to attempting to resolve the issue, the user will have a better understanding of the relevant issues to be resolved. The more important the issue, the more the user is encouraged by the DSS to use a formal approach in defining the issue.

Use of a formal issue definition process leads to a more rigorous definition of the issue. The effort to create a well-defined issue causes users to develop a better understanding of the issue than they might attain without a DSS. Better issue definitions and the concomitant improved understanding of the issues should lead to an improved identification of the preferred response to resolve each issue.

### Improved Definitions of Relevant Issues

Good issue definitions should lead to a better appreciation of what is required to resolve the issue than situations in which the decision maker does not have a good understanding of the issue. Also, by offering a formal process for formulating alternative actions to resolve the issue, then more potential responses can be identified.

The DSS then offers different methods for eliminating and rank-ordering the alternatives. Developing a good issue definition, identifying many alternative responses, and culling and rank-ordering the alternatives should lead to better actions to resolve each existing or predicted issue.

### Improved Issue Resolution

The final part of decision making involves the implementation of the decision. In cases in which the people or mechanisms required to resolve an issue are connected to the decision maker's computer, the computer can be used to transmit the appropriate portion of the total resolution process to the proper individuals or mechanisms.

## Improved Implementation of Decisions

Only when many organizational decision makers keep good records of their decision processes and outcomes while using the DSS described here, will it be known for sure how beneficial the DSS is. Even then, the resulting conclusions may be debatable. However, it seems logical that computer-supported decision making that is behaviorally responsive and that improves the definition of issues and formalizes the determination of a preferred response must result in better decision making in the sense that response outcomes will be better than without the DSS.

## WHERE TO GO FROM HERE

Organizations that are interested in acquiring a DSS as described in this book must wait for some vendor to develop such a system, find a contractor willing to develop a system, or have an internal group create such a system.

## Acquiring a Decision Support System

It appears that today the idea of improved decision support has come to mean improved manipulation of databases. However, that is a small part, and perhaps much less relevant than the other parts of the decision process. Until well-designed, behaviorally oriented, user-friendly DSSs that actually improve the user's decision-making abilities are provided to decision makers, then the promise of computer-assisted decision making in modern organizations may remain elusive and unattainable.

## Build or Buy?

Since there is no vendor offering of the type of DSS proposed here, customers will have to acquire this kind of DSS from software vendors who are able to create a specific system to meet the needs of each particular organization. Hopefully, in the not-too-distant future, behaviorally oriented DSSs will be offered as COTS packages at reasonable prices.

Taking an inappropriate approach to creating a DSS can be very expensive for a large organization. The point is illustrated in the movie *Casablanca*. Claude Raines (the police chief) asks Humphrey Bogart (Rick), "Why did you come to Casablanca?"

Rick responds, "For the waters." The police chief says, "But there are no waters here. Casablanca is a desert." To which Rick replies, "I was misinformed."

If an organization is truly interested in acquiring a behaviorally responsive DSS, perhaps this book will keep the organizational leader from being misinformed.

# Appendix A:
# Decision Rules

## INTRODUCTION

This appendix contains an overview description of the alternative methods that can be used for making decisions regarding the selection of alternatives (Sage, 1981; 1990). To make a decision, the decision maker uses decision rules, either consciously or unconsciously. These decision rules can be divided into three areas:

1. comparative elimination,
2. systematic evaluation, and
3. personal judgment.

Decision rules allow the user to cull (i.e., eliminate) and rank-order options, that is, to systematically decompose and evaluate the issue so as to identify the preferred option. Comparative rules are used for performing comparisons of alternatives, such as alternative solutions to an issue. Comparisons are usually performed to eliminate one or more alternatives. However, the user can continue the process until only one alternative is left, in which case comparisons can be used to actually select the preferred alternative. There is a possibility that use of a comparison method in this manner can lead to the selection of an alternative that actually is not the preferred one if certain conditions exist. Therefore, care should be exercised in implementing comparison rules and the user should check the final outcome for a resulting solution that does not seem to be correct.

## COMPARISON RULES

There are four basic methods for making comparisons: (a) comparison against a standard, (b) comparison across attributes, (c) comparison within attributes, and (d) judgmental comparison.

## COMPARISON AGAINST A STANDARD

There are two types of the Comparison Against a Standard decision rule: disjunctive and conjunctive.

- **Disjunctive Comparison**
  The decision maker identifies minimally acceptable standards for each relevant attribute, so that alternatives that pass the critical standard of one or more attributes are retained. Alternatives are rejected only if they fail to exceed all of the critical standards. This type of comparison can be easily computed as follows:

    If $x_j \geq c_j$ (or $x_j \leq c_j$ as the specific case may be) for at least one $j = 1, 2, \ldots$, m; then accept the alternative,

  where $x_j$ is the value for the $j^{th}$ attribute and $c_j$ is the value for the $j^{th}$ reference standard. The case is that $x_j < c_j$ (or $>$ as the specific case may be) for all values of j for the alternative to be rejected.

    This rule is noncompensatory. A compensatory approximation to a disjunctive decision rule for attributes $x_j$ is

$$U = \Sigma_j \ 1/\{(1 + x_j/c_j)n_j\}, \ n_j \gg 1, \text{for } j = 1, 2, \ldots, m; \qquad (A.1)$$

  where m is the number of attributes and $c_j$ is the critical value on attribute $x_j$. If $U > 1$, then the alternative in question is retained.

    A compensatory rule is one where an excess capability in one attribute can be used to compensate for a deficit capability in another attribute. Usually, the Comparison Against a Standard decision rule is not the compensatory version.

- **Conjunctive Comparison**
  The decision maker identifies minimally acceptable standards for each relevant attribute, so that alternatives that pass the critical standard of all attributes are retained. Alternatives are rejected if they fail to meet or exceed a single minimum standard. This type of comparison can be easily computed as follows:

If $x_j \geq c_j$ (or $x_j \leq c_j$ as the specific case may be) for all $j = 1, 2, \ldots$, m; then accept the alternative,

where $x_j$ is the value for the $j^{th}$ attribute and $c_j$ is the value for the $j^{th}$ reference standard.

    If $x_j < c_j$ (or $>$ as the specific case may be) for just one value of j, then the alternative is rejected. A compensatory approximation to a disjunctive decision rule for attributes $x_j$ is

$$U = \Pi_j \ 1/\{(1 + c_j/x_j)n_j\}, \ n_j \gg 1, \text{for } j = 1, 2, \ldots, m; \qquad (A.2)$$

where m is the number of attributes and $c_j$ is the critical value on attribute $x_j$. Retain the alternative if U is greater than a number slightly less than 1, say 0.99.

By iterating through the conjunctive acceptance and disjunctive rejection rules several times with adjustable critical values, the disjunctive and conjunctive comparison rules form a set of satisficing rules.

As an example, suppose a person wants to buy a car and has decided on three attributes the car will be judged on: a) price, b) miles per gallon, and c) comfort. Suppose this person decides that the price must be less than $20,000; the miles per gallon must be at least 30; and the comfort must be excellent or better on a poor, good, excellent, and exceptional scale. This person finds a car, car A, that is priced at $17,500; the miles per gallon is 27; and the comfort is excellent. Then a noncompensatory conjunctive comparison against the standard is

$17,500 < $20,000 (so price is okay)
27 < 30 (so mileage is not okay because in this case > was appropriate),      (A.3)
and excellent $\geq$ excellent (so comfort is okay).

So car A would be rejected as a candidate. Now suppose that car B has the following qualities: a) price is $19,000, b) mileage is 31, and c) comfort is excellent. Then a conjunctive comparison is:

$19,000 < $20,000 (so price is okay)
31 > 30 (so mileage is okay)      (A.4)
excellent $\geq$ excellent (so comfort is okay).

So car B is accepted as a candidate. Note that inequalities can often be changed if that is desired. For example, by using gallons per mile (which is 1/miles per gallon), the comparison would be,

1/(mileage of car B) < standard (= 1/30)

which would be okay since 1/31 < 1/30 and 31 miles per gallon is better than 30 miles per gallon.

## COMPARISON ACROSS ATTRIBUTES

There are two types of Comparison Across Attributes rules: dominance and additive difference.

- **Dominance**
  Choose alternative $a_1$ over $a_2$ if $a_1$ is better than $a_2$ on at least one aspect and not worse than $a_2$ on any other aspect, where an aspect is the score of a specific attention on a specific attribute. Sometimes this is called Pareto dominance.

Using the same example as above, it is clear that neither car dominates the other, since

| Car B | | Car A |
|---|---|---|
| 1/$19,000 | < | 1/$17,500 |
| 31 | > | 27 |
| excellent | ≥ | excellent |

$$(A.5)$$

where ≥ is required on all parameters and > on at least one in order for Car B to dominate Car A.

- **Additive Difference**

  For alternatives $a_1$ and $a_2$, compute the value differences $U_j(a_1) - U_j(a_2)$ where $U_j$ is the value for the $j^{th}$ attribute for $j = 1, 2, \ldots, m$. Elicit the weight, $f_j[U_j(a_1) - U_j(a_2)]$, for each difference from the decision maker, where $-1.0 \leq f_j[\bullet] \leq 1.0$. This means that the decision maker likes $a_1$ better if $U > 0$ and likes $a_2$ better if $U < 0$, where,

$$U = \Sigma_j \, f_j[U_j(a_1) - U_j(a_2)].$$   (A.6)

If $U = 0$, then the method is indeterminate. This is a compensatory rule.

For the two cars, assume that Car A and Car B are given the following values for cost, mileage, and comfort, as shown below:

| Car A | Car B |
|---|---|
| 0.95 | 0.85 |
| 0.75 | 0.90 |
| 0.90 | 0.90 |

Then U(Car A, Car B) = [0.95 – 0.85] + [0.75 – 0.90] + [0.90 – 0.90] = –0.05. So Car B is preferred.

## COMPARISON WITHIN ATTRIBUTES

There are three types of rules for comparison within attributes: a) lexicographic, b) elimination by aspects, and c) maximizing number of desirable attributes. In these cases, no minimum performance level is established, since comparisons of alternatives are made relative to one another.

- **Lexicographic Rules**

  Make the option selection based on the alternative with the most desirable attribute in sequential order, beginning with the most important attribute, then the next most important attribute, and so forth. Sometimes a delta difference is used so that an alternative's attribute value is not considered better unless it is greater than an *a priori* difference $\Delta_j$. This rule, with the delta difference, is a type of fuzzy logic approach. This rule is called lexicographic because it orders alternatives in a manner exactly like words are alphabetically ordered in a dictionary.

In this case, if the critical attribute is miles per gallon, then car B is selected as a candidate over car A. If price were the most important attribute, then car A would be selected over car B as a potential candidate. If comfort were the most important attribute, then the next most important attribute would have to be used since both cars have the same comfort value (i.e., excellent).

- **Elimination by Aspects**

Attributes are assumed to have different importance weights. For some alternatives, select an attribute with a probability that is proportional to its weight. Alternatives which do not have attribute scores above this reference value are eliminated. For some remaining alternatives, select an attribute with probability proportional to its weight and perform the evaluation again. Continue the evaluation process until a single alternative is left. This rule is similar to the lexicographic method except the selection mechanism is based on a probabilistic analogy.

For this rule, create a table (Table A.1) as follows assigning the denoted probabilities to each attribute so that the attributes can be ordered. Identify an aspiration level for the price as $20,000. Reject the alternative if price of car A or B is greater than the aspiration level. Both pass this comparison. Assign an aspiration level of 30 miles per gallon for mileage. In this case, the test for miles per gallon must show a mileage greater than 30 for the next most important (probable) attribute. Thus, car A is eliminated and car B is retained as a candidate.

- **Maximizing Number of Desirable Attributes**

Given any two alternatives, for each attribute rate the attribute value as equal or better, or worse than the other alternative's attribute value. Select the alternative that has the greatest number of attributes with a favorable classification.

For this rule, car B has 2 desirable attributes relative to car A, and car A also has 2 desirable attributes relative to car B. This method is indeterminate for this case.

**TABLE A.1.**
**Probabilities and Attributes**

| Probability | Car A | Car B | Aspiration level | Passing test |
|---|---|---|---|---|
| 0.5 (price) | $17,000 | $19,000 | $20,000 | ≤ |
| 0.3 (mileage) | 27 | 31 | 30 | ≥ |
| 0.2 (comfort) | excellent | excellent | excellent | ≥ |

This method as stated is ordinal. If it were made to be a cardinal comparison, then the percentage of excess performance could be determined and accumulated. In this manner, the cumulative excess could be used to compare the alternatives. Ordinal and cardinal relationships are explained later.

## JUDGMENTAL COMPARISON

The method is based on the user's own judgment for eliminating alternatives. The user simply examines the alternatives and based on his feeling, decides that one or more alternatives are not worth further consideration and can be eliminated. Unless the user is experienced at doing this sort of thing, one's intuition may not be accurate and that is the reason for the more formal methods explained in this appendix.

## STRUCTURED EVALUATION OF ALTERNATIVES

Systematic rules are methods that depend on a set of well-defined steps. A favorite method for rank-ordering alternatives is the multiattribute utility analysis (MAUT). These rules are frequently referred to as "normative rules." Evaluation rules allow the decision maker to rank-order alternative actions so that the preferred or "best" one, in the opinion of the user, can be recognized.

The theories for the various systematic rules are based on rather strict assumptions and hypotheses for the implementation of a specific rule (Fishburn, 1970). The identification of the attributes of the alternatives should consider that they should be preferentially independent. That is, the attributes should be identified and selected such that the assessed value assigned to any attribute should not be affected by, nor affect, the values assigned to the other attributes. Weights are the importance factors assigned to each attribute and should sum to one. The objective of a systematic rule is to assign a numerical value or utility ($U(A_i)$) to each option $A_i$ such that if,

$$U(A_j) > U(A_k) \text{ for any } j \text{ and } k, \text{ then the option } A_j \text{ is said to be preferred to } A_k. \quad (A.7)$$

Systematic rules require that the problem be decomposed into its elements, namely, the environmental states that can result, the objectives for the options, an evaluation of the effects of the options, the alternative options, the attributes of the options, the weight for each attribute, or the rating levels for the values given to each attribute's worth to the user for each option.

The MAUT approach requires that the user decompose the problem features on which utility is based into a number, m, of components called attributes. The attribute decomposition is in the form of a tree whose nodes are the quantified values elicited from appropriate sources based on the values for the lowest level attributes. For example, the weights for evaluating a car might be arranged as shown in

Figure A.1, assuming that the principal attributes are cost, comfort, and style. The attributes and subattributes are shown along with the concomitant weights as might be elicited from a user. The lowest level attributes are cost of car, resale value, miles per dollar, maintenance, interior comfort, shocks, chassis, springs, body style, dashboard style, floorboard design, and seat design. When these are properly weighted and assigned values, then the utility of the car can be determined.

Weights for each attribute must be elicited and the additive form of the utility of an option $a_i$ is

$$U(a_i) = \Sigma_j \; w_j \bullet v_j(a_i) \text{ where } j = 1, 2, \ldots, n; \text{ where } \Sigma_j \; w_j = 1; \qquad \text{(A.8)}$$

and where $w_j$ is the weight of the $j^{th}$ attribute, $v_j(a_i)$ is the value or score of the $j^{th}$ attribute for alternative option $a_i$. The weight values (or utilities) are elicited from the user.

Weights should always be normalized so that they will sum to one by making $w_j = w_j'/\Sigma_j \; w_j'$ where $w_j'$ is the original weight value such that $\Sigma_j \; w_j' \neq 1$. Using linear models in which weights and values are chosen by nonoptimal methods (often because that is the only method possible with the existing data), it has been shown that when the parameters of the model are chosen properly, a simple linear model like equation (A.8) may outperform an expert (Dawes, 1979).

A simple example of an application of the MAUT approach would be a manager who notices that the mail system in the organization is very slow (issue detection). She defines the problem as follows: "The organization personnel assigned to receive, process, and distribute incoming mail are requiring an excessive amount of time." She finds out that there are two major time functions of the internal mail system:

1.   the time to scan and sort incoming mail, and
2.   the time to deliver the mail to organization personnel.

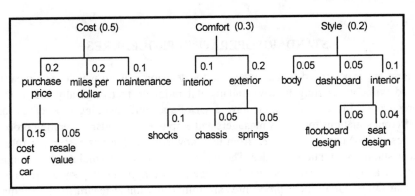

**FIGURE A.1.   Hierarchical attributes for evaluating a car.**

She discovers that the first time function (for scanning and sorting) is two-thirds of the problem. She believes that the problem can be satisfactorily resolved by creating an improved scanning and sorting procedure.

There are two candidates: Process 1 and Process 2. Process 1 takes 10 seconds per mail item and costs $1000, and Process 2 takes 20 seconds per mail item and costs $800. She uses a multiattribute utility analysis and assigns 70% of the weight to the time attribute and 30% to the cost attribute. She uses the following multiattribute utility analysis equation:

$$U(P_i) = 0.7 \; (V_i(time)) + 0.3 \; (V_i(cost)) \qquad (A.9)$$

where $U(P_i)$ is the utility of the $i^{th}$ alternative process $P_i$, and $V_i$ is the value given to the attributes *time* and *cost* for process i. She decides that,

$$V_1(10 \text{ seconds}) = 0.9 \text{ and } V_1(\$1000) = 0.9, \text{ and} \qquad (A.10)$$

$$V_2(20 \text{ seconds}) = 0.5 \text{ and } V_2(\$800) = 1.0, \text{ so that} \qquad (A.11)$$

$$U(P_1) = 0.63 + 0.27 = 0.90 \text{ and } U(P_2) = 0.35 + 0.30 = 0.65. \qquad (A.12)$$

So the manager chooses Process 1 as her preferred alternative since $U(P_1) > U(P_2)$.

## PERSONAL JUDGMENT

Personal judgment rules are the methods that people use that are based on experience. They consist of standard operating procedures, intuitive affect, and reasoning by analogy. Judgment rules allow the user to select the preferred alternative based on an examination of the situation and concomitant options as a whole and go with their "gut feeling."

## STANDARD OPERATING PROCEDURES

These are experienced-based guidelines for decision making which are typically used without resorting to any fundamental rationale that originally led to the procedures. Most organizations have a set of standard operating procedures for different situations for use by managers and employees. Standard operating procedures (SOPs) can be developed from the knowledge and use of systematic rules, heuristic rules, and holistic rules. These procedures can be formulated by a single person assigned by an upper-level manager, or by a group of people within an organization. Often these procedures are followed without regard to the original rationale used to develop them. However, this is not recommended always, since the user should question the procedures if they do not seem to be appropriate (Argyris, 1982).

SOPs are sometimes implicit, such as when they are spread by word of mouth throughout the organization. This can frequently mean that many employees are not aware of the procedures or at least not all of them, and may even forget some that they have heard. These procedures are sometimes delineated in a manual which might be titled "Standard Operating Policies and Procedures." This manual should describe the procedures and may give examples of situations in which the procedures should be applied.

When embedded in a DSS, the SOPs can be made available with ease to all users of the DSS. The SOPs can be automated as an expert subsystem so that the DSS can quickly recommend an action in response to a situation identified by the computer or as provided by the user. The procedures can be considered a dynamic entity so that as users find errors in the procedures they can appropriately modify them with consensual agreement within the organization or provide suggested modifications to the programming department.

SOPs are especially useful to users who are novices to the organization rules and are not yet familiar with the relevant environment or the SOPs. Whatever these procedures turn out to be, they should be minimal. The more procedures in the manual, the more opportunities there are to slow things down and to get management and subordinates hot and bothered (Peters, 1987). In fact, the fewer the procedures in the manual, the more freedom organizational decision makers will have in making their choices for resolving the issues. However, once the SOPs are reflected in an expert system, the detail or number of procedures should not be detrimental to the organization. In fact, it seems that detailed SOPs would be of benefit to the organization, provided the organization wished to maintain fairly tight control over the approaches to resolving issues. However, many organizations intentionally keep SOPs to a minimum in hopes that employees will utilize their creative skills in solving relevant issues.

The lack of organizational procedural knowledge and the inability to recognize situations in which specific procedures apply are some limitations of the use of these procedures. When these procedures have been learned so well that they become a natural response process, then they can be used for skill-based decision making. However, these procedures can be stored in the DSS as an expert subsystem and used to support rule-based decision making as a set of decision rules.

## INTUITIVE AFFECT

Selections are made based on the whole picture of a situation. Valuation is usually based on an attempt to determine whether alternatives are pleasant or unpleasant, likeable or unlikeable, or good or bad for the decision maker. That is, how do decision makers feel about the alternatives, based on their education, experience, and other aspects of their personalities or cognitive modes? It emphasizes the uniqueness of personalistic value judgments. Intuitive affect is often used by experienced people when deciding on an option.

## REASONING BY ANALOGY

Reasoning by analogy is accomplished by making a selection from among alternatives based on the use of analogies, prototypes, or other models that have been developed from experiences that allow a person to feel familiar with the situation. Many scientific authors (e.g., Sage, 1981) claim that reasoning by analogy is the basis for hypothesis generation. However, hypothesis generation is probably more akin to abductive reasoning than inductive reasoning. The use of analogic reasoning, as the other holistic processes, is contingent upon the context, that is, the environment, the situation, and the task.

## SUMMARY

Whatever the choice on deciding how to decide, the decision maker is faced with considerations such as time limitations, cost limitations, complexity of the situation, risks, and the importance of the decision.

# Appendix B:
# Commercial Expert System

## INTRODUCTION

Below is a HyperTalk description of the Commercial Expert System as programmed for the *DSS Demo* HyperCard system. The data for the environment are described by (a) the slope of the company's sales level, (b) the slope of the competitor's sales level, (c) the slope of the overall sales level, and (d) whether the consumer desires a better product or not.

## THE EXPERT SYSTEM

The system will yield the following resolutions for differing descriptions of the environment:

Situation A (steady, increasing, steady, yes) or Situation B (decreasing, increasing, steady, yes)
   Put new product team to work creating a better product.

Situation C (steady, increasing, increasing, yes) or Situation D (decreasing, decreasing, increasing, yes)
   Put "skunk works" team to work to quickly create a better product.

Situation E (increasing, -, -, no)
   Continue with current plans.

Situation F (decreasing, steady, increasing, yes) or Situation G (decreasing, decreasing, increasing, yes)
   Put "skunk works" team to work to quickly create a better product.

145

## COMMERCIAL EXPERT SYSTEM

put word 1 of line 1 of card field "environment state" into w
put word 1 of line 2 of card field "environment state" into x
put word 1 of line 3 of card field "environment state" into y
put word 1 of line 4 of card field "environment state" into z
put "No Case" into card field "response"

if w = "steady" and x = "increasing" and y = "steady" and z = "yes" or w =
"decreasing" and x = "increasing" and y = "steady" and z = "yes" then
    put "Put new product team to work creating a better product." into card field
    "response"
end if

if w = "steady" and x = "increasing" and y = "increasing" and z = "yes" or w =
"decreasing" and x = "decreasing" and y = "increasing" and z = "yes" then
    put "Put 'skunk works' team to work to quickly create a better product." into card
    field "response"
end if

if w = "increasing" and z = "no" then
    put "Continue with current plans." into card field "response"
end if

if w = "decreasing" and x = "steady" and y = "increasing" and z = "yes" or w =
"decreasing" and x = "decreasing" and y = "increasing" and z = "yes" then
    put "Put 'skunk works' team to work to quickly create a better product." into card
    field "response"
end if

# Appendix C:
# Human Biases

## INTRODUCTION

Many human errors are characterized as biases. There are many types of human biases, a few of which are listed as follows (Sage, 1981):

*Adjustment and anchoring*—This occurs when a person finds that problem-solving difficulties are due not to the lack of data and information, but rather to the existence of excess data and information. In these situations the person may resort to heuristics, which may reduce the effort required to arrive at a solution. In using this heuristic, the person selects a particular data point, such as the mean, as an initial or starting point, or anchor, and then adjusts that value improperly to incorporate the rest of the data so as to result in a flawed information analysis.

*Illusion of Control*—A decision maker may believe that a good outcome in a chance situation resulted from a good decision, which may well have been a poor decision. The decision maker may then assume a feeling of control over events that is not reasonable.

*Illusion of Correlation*—A mistaken belief that two events covary when they do not.

*Desire for self-fulfilling prophecies*—A person may value a certain result, interpretation, or conclusion, and acquire and analyze only information that supports this conclusion.

*Conservatism*—This results from a failure to revise estimates as much as they should be revised, based on receipt of new significant information.

*Fact-value confusion*—A person may have strongly held values which may often be regarded and presented as facts. Only the type of information that confirms or lends credibility to one's views and values is sought.

*Selective perceptions*—A person may seek only information that confirms his views and values. He will disregard or ignore disconfirming evidence. Issues are structured on the basis of personal experience and wishful thinking. There are many illustrations of selective perception, such as "reading between the lines." An example of this is the person who will recount a story (perhaps apocryphal) of how a man not wearing a seat belt was thrown from his car in a head-on collision and landed in a haystack unharmed, thus ignoring all the factual evidence confirming the added safety of wearing a seat belt.

*Hindsight*—A person is unable to think objectively if he receives information that an outcome has occurred and he is told to ignore this information. With hindsight, outcomes that have occurred will seem to have been inevitable. Relationships are more easily seen in hindsight than in foresight and some people will find it easy to change their predictions after the fact to correspond to what is known to have occurred.

*Law of small numbers*—This bias is committed by people who are insufficiently sensitive to the quality of evidence. They often express greater confidence in predictions based on small samples of data with confirming evidence than in much larger samples with minor disconfirming evidence. Sample size and reliability often have little influence on confidence.

*Redundancy*—Some people have more confidence in their predictions when there is redundancy in the data, even though this overconfidence is usually not warranted.

*Overconfidence*—Some people generally ascribe more credibility to data than is warranted and hence overestimate the probability of success merely due to the presence of an abundance of data. The greater the amount of data, the more confident the person is in the accuracy of the data.

*Availability*—A decision maker may use only easily available information and ignore pertinent information that requires an extra effort to attain. An event is believed to occur frequently or with high probability if it is easy to recall similar events.

*Order effects*—Sometimes the order in which data are presented will affect information retention in memory. The first piece of data presented (primacy effect) and the last presented (recency effect) will assume undue importance in the mind of the decision maker.

*Representativeness*—Some people, when making inferences from data, give too much weight to results of small samples. As sample size is increased, the results of small samples are taken to be representative of the larger population. The "laws" of representativeness differ considerably from the laws of probability and violations of the conjunction rule:

$$P(A \cap B) \geq P(A) \text{ are often observed,}$$

where $P(A \cap B)$ means the probability of events A and B.

*Habit*—Sometimes familiarity with a particular procedure for solving a problem may result in reuse of the same procedure and selection of the same alternative when confronted with a similar type of problem and similar information. An alternative is chosen because it was previously believed to be acceptable for a perceived similar purpose or because of superstition.

*Ease of recall*—Data that can be easily recalled or accessed will affect perception of the likelihood of similar events occurring again. Some people will weigh data that can be easily recalled more in their decision processes than data which cannot be easily recalled.

*Wishful Thinking*—Sometimes the decision maker cannot differentiate between fact and fiction, causing preferences by the decision maker for poor alternatives. These decisions assume outcomes based on irrational or unsubstantiated assumptions.

*Expectations*—Sometimes the decision maker will remember and attach higher validity to information that confirms their previously held beliefs than they do to disconfirming information. The user may ignore disconfirming information by collecting much information that will include data that are desired for confirming poor choices.

## DISCUSSION

Two examples of human bias error are presented to illustrate how poor decisions can be made when available data are ignored. The first story, which is true but apocryphal, concerns a company that had recently installed a new, expensive mainframe computer system. After considering the significant cost of a voltage surge protector and the small likelihood that a bolt of lightning might strike near enough to disable the computer, the company decided to forego a surge protector that would minimize the damage to the computer in case of lightning or other voltage surge phenomena. Within 6 months of the computer installation, during a severe thunder storm—which was a common occurrence in the area—a bolt of lightning struck near the company building and knocked out the computer system for several days. It cost the company dearly in money and lost computer support to repair the system.

Recalling that the probability for this occurrence was considered to be very small, the company then decided not to install a surge protector, since the likelihood of a highly unlikely event (as perceived by the company) recurring again in the near-term future was indeed very small (even smaller than before the first lightning strike). Two weeks after the repair, during another severe thunder storm, a bolt of lightning again struck near the building and the computer system was again disabled for several days. At this point the company decided to install the surge protector. Just think of the considerable expense and inconvenience of two computer outages because of the decision to save a few bucks by not buying a surge protector.

Another true case involved the purchase of a mainframe computer by a company. The company wanted to replace its existing mainframe with a new system that could support remote terminals for both scientific and business accounting problems. An artificially detailed study was performed, with the computer systems manager and the company president serving as the lead analysts. Much data were collected but no analytical process was created or followed. Also, although inputs from knowledgeable people within the company were solicited, these inputs were summarily ignored. When the time came to select a computer system, the two decision makers selected a system that made no sense to those knowledgeable people whose advice had been requested and ignored. The selected system turned out to be very inadequate for the job. A minimum one-year lease was signed and at the end of the lease year, a different system was leased to replace the inappropriate system.

Both these true incidents are examples of situations in which human bias error (wishful thinking and selective perceptions, respectively) had caused poor decisions. Even a nominal knowledge of decision-making processes could have been used to avoid such poor decisions, were the decision makers aware of the proper methods and willing to learn a better approach.

There are many examples of such biases. It would be too difficult to check for each one while going through the data gathering process. However, the decision maker should be aware of the possibility of human biases and especially his own biases. Most people are not aware of their biases unless they have made a serious effort to detect them and then to consciously diminish their effects when making decisions.

# Appendix D:
# A Formal Approach to Creating Issue Definitions

## INTRODUCTION

During the generation of the alternative hypotheses, the user may wish to begin with informal, or implicit, hypotheses. Informal hypotheses can be developed based on the initial issue definition and a method for keeping account of the alternatives, if the client should care for such formality. A formal approach might provide a method for storing alternative hypotheses and evidence sets for future reference and to provide rationale for later arguments. However, users may wish to use common everyday language for developing the informal initial issue definitions as well as the final definitions.

Explicit or formal hypotheses may be based on converting the informal hypotheses to a Toulmin format (Toulmin, 1958; Toulmin, Reike, & Janik, 1979). In formal form, hypotheses can be checked for logic validity using an assumption-based truth maintenance system (ATMS) (de Kleer, 1986). Formal hypotheses should also be checked for mutual exclusiveness and reasonable exhaustiveness. This is a subjective process and is essentially based on the assessment that each hypothesis cannot occur when another hypothesis occurs. The exhaustiveness is declared when no new hypothesis can be identified or when cost and time constraints prohibit further activity on this task. The gamut of hypotheses forms the *frame of discernment* of the issue.

## TOULMIN ARGUMENTS

For formal hypotheses, a reasoning structure can be developed that consists of six parts (Mason & Mitroff, 1981):

1. *claim* is the conclusion of the statement;
2. *grounds* provide the basis, data, and/or theory for the claim;
3. *warrant* is an argument that justifies the grounds;
4. *backing* is the body of evidence or information that supports the warrant;
5. *modal qualifier* is a qualifier that supposes a counter to the warrant's validity; and
6. *possible rebuttal* is the body of evidence that provides support to counter the warrant.

The resulting structure of logical reasoning and inferencing of Figure D.1 provides a very useful framework for the study of human information processing activities. This is so because it provides an explicit, structured model of logical reasoning that is suited for analytical inquiry and computer implementation.

Toulmin's arguments are either a tautology or an inference (Toulmin, 1958). Tautologies are true by definition since they are only a restatement of a given fact. Inferences are conclusions that are generated by a series of linked facts or assertions in a hierarchical manner. Inferences require warrants and hence are never conclusively true. The belief value of the claim can be determined from the basic probability assignments (or other forms of uncertainty) of input evidence, which act directly on either the backing or rebuttal in the argument and in turn affect the prior beliefs of each element in the Toulmin net. Evidence may either confirm or disconfirm the backing or rebuttal.

A Toulmin structured argument would appear as follows: *Given that* grounds is true *because* warrant is true *since* backing is true, *so probably* claim is true *unless* rebuttal is true. For complex arguments, the claim of one subargument is the output of data, warrant, or backing for another subargument. Toulmin's framework assists in identifying the role of assumptions in making an argument so that questions concerning the assumptions can be addressed, such as

- What assumptions are being made?
- At what level are these assumptions being made?
- How acceptable are the assumptions?

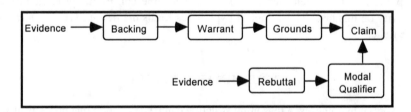

**FIGURE D.1.**  Simple Toulmin net for logic check or inferencing.

- Can the argument be destroyed on the basis of a counter to any of the assumptions?
- Can the assumptions be removed or better supported?
- Are the warrants properly supported?
- Have we argued against the rebuttals properly?
- Should the claim or supporting arguments be modified because of rebuttals?

Through the linking of subarguments to other subarguments in the development of the entire argument for a particular claim that defines a problem or issue, one has a chained argument that can be used to respond to challenges to the argument. In this way, Toulmin's framework serves as a model for making arguments to support any decision perspective of interest, such as political, societal, or technical. A complete Toulmin network can be a simple Toulmin net or a connection of many Toulmin nets (complex net), so that a warrant or grounds could be supported by another Toulmin net, and some part of the supporting net, say the rebuttal, could be supported by another Toulmin net, and so forth.

The warrants in the proof of an asserted reference can be categorized into one of three types: substantive, authoritative, or motivational arguments (Smith, 1992):

1. *Substantive arguments* are logical arguments that verify a claim by means of the application of logic to the movement from data to claim.
2. *Authoritative arguments* are ethical arguments and verify a claim by reviewing the credentials of the source of the statement, its general veracity, and its credibility, based on data from a reliable and credible source.
3. *Motivational arguments* are pathetic arguments and appeal to the feelings of pity, sorrow, compassion, or sympathy. The claim is verified by examining one's own needs, values, and aspirations to see if they are shared by others.

## SUBSTANTIVE ARGUMENTS

These arguments comprise six basic relationships: generalization, classification, cause and effect, sign or symptom, parallel case, and analogy.

1. *Generalization* is the extension of the specific to the general.
2. *Classification* is the opposite of generalization.
3. *Cause and effect* is the relating of results to observations.
4. *Sign or symptom* argument is when a sign exists that indicates some effect.
5. *Parallel case* is an assertion that an item is essentially similar to an item in the problem.
6. *Analogy* is an argument that asserts that a general relationship is essentially similar to a relationship found between two items in the problem.

## AUTHORITATIVE ARGUMENTS

These arguments are based on reports, statements of fact, or expert opinions, and are accepted as true because of their source's veracity or esteem. The grounds for the authoritative warrant can be achieved in one or more of the following five ways:

1. *Expertise.* Show that the source is knowledgeable in the area of consideration.
2. *Method.* Show that the source used an acceptable and well-known method for arriving at the conclusion.
3. *Consensus.* Show that the source's conclusions are the same as those derived from several other sources.
4. *Tradition.* Show that since something was always accepted as true in the past it should be accepted as true now.
5. *Basic belief.* Show that the source's statement is based on a fundamental belief or tenant, such as a religious conviction.

## MOTIVATIONAL ARGUMENTS

These arguments appeal to the basic values or mores of the listener for their validity. The appeal is to a basic human motive, such as physiological, safety, social, esteem, or self-actualization, in terms of its social value (such as justice, liberty, equality, and truth). The motivational argument may assert either that a certain value should be placed upon a person, event, object, or thing in the problem, or that a certain alternative option should (or should not) be selected.

It may be useful to be able to identify motivational arguments, since they are often used when substantive or authoritative arguments should be used. Usually, a person should avoid using these types of arguments, since they can easily be disconfirmed.

## QUANTIFYING ARGUMENTS

The introduction of the rebuttal, usually through a dialectic, causes one to have to consider alternative possibilities, including the possibility that the claim is not true (Smith, 1992). Suppose one has a claim C that says that statement A is true and there exists grounds G that supports the claim. Additionally, there exists a model M that shows that C is true when G is input to the model, i.e., $M(G) \Rightarrow C$ or simply using the model M it follows that, $G \Rightarrow C$ when G is true where "$\Rightarrow$" means "implies."

Now suppose there is a counterclaim or rebuttal that says, $R \Rightarrow \sim C$ if R is true where "$\sim C$" means "not C." The *modus ponens* syllogism says that if $G \Rightarrow C$ is true, and G is true, then C is true or in another form, the logical expression $[(G \Rightarrow C) \wedge G]$ is the same as $[G \wedge C]$ where $\wedge$ is the logical conjunctive operator, that is, it means "and." If a rebuttal logic expression [(R $\Rightarrow$ ~C) $\wedge$ R] is added to [G $\wedge$ C], then if the rebuttal is expressed as [~C], we get [(G $\wedge$ C) $\wedge$ ~C], which is [G $\wedge$ (C $\wedge$ ~C)]. But C $\wedge$ ~C is a contradiction so that something in the expression must not be true. However, if the various statements are not considered as completely true or completely false, then the various terms in the claims expression as well as the rebuttal expression can be retained, with the interpretation that a rebuttal simply weakens the claim but does not necessarily repudiate it.

An analysis method developed by Rescher and Manor and explained in Mason and Mitroff (1981) uses the concept of plausibility. The first concept is the notion of a *maximally consistent subset*, which is formed as follows:

1. Information:
   a)  A set of data or grounds G.
   b)  An inference model G $\Rightarrow$ C.
   c)  A claim C.
   d)  A rebuttal ~C.
2. Epistemic (or knowledge) policies and maximally consistent subsets:
   a)  $P_a$ = {G $\wedge$ [G $\Rightarrow$ C] $\wedge$ C}, i.e., accept the data, model, and claim as true.
   b)  $P_b$ = {G $\wedge$ ~C}, i.e., accept the data and the counterclaim as true.
   c)  $P_c$ = {[G $\Rightarrow$ C] $\wedge$ ~C}, i.e., accept the model and the counterclaim as true.

A maximally consistent subset (MCS) is the largest set of propositions that can be conjoined such that the resulting subset remains consistent. There are three MCSs for the four assertions G, G $\Rightarrow$ C, C, and ~C, *viz.*, the $P_a$, $P_b$, and $P_c$ above. Each of the MCSs gives rise to a different epistemic policy (i.e., a basis from which a set of knowledge or an argument is chosen). To accept $P_a$ is to accept the argument as given. The policy $P_b$ says to accept (G $\wedge$ ~C). If one chooses to accept $P_c$ then one is accepting both the model G $\Rightarrow$ C and the rebuttal R $\Rightarrow$ ~C as well. The logical conclusion of this acceptance is (~G $\wedge$ ~C). Thus an epistemic policy is the acceptance and rejection of the elements of the argument that are used to argue a claim, as well as the acceptance or rejection of a claim.

To select the proper MCS, the overall plausibility of the subset is determined from the plausibility of it elements. Plausibility refers to the credibility of an argument. Plausibility can be measured on a scale like the one shown in Table D.1.

**TABLE D.1.**
**Plausibility Scale**

| 0 | 1 | 2 | 3 | 4 | 5 |
|---|---|---|---|---|---|
| Logical truth | High plausibility | Moderate plausibility | Low plausibility | Very low plausibility | No plausibility |

Thus smaller numbers relate to higher plausibilities. Suppose that the plausibilities $p[X]$ for the four assertions are: $p[G] = 1$, $p[G \Rightarrow C] = 4$, $p[C] = 2$, and $p[\sim C] = 3$.

The plausibilities of the MCSs can be computed as an average of the elemental plausibilities as follows:

$$p[P_a] = (p[G] + p[G \Rightarrow C] + p[C])/3 = (1 + 4 + 2)/3 = 2.33 \qquad (D.1)$$

$$p[P_b] = (p[G] + p[\sim C])/2 = (1 + 3)/2 = 2.00 \qquad (D.2)$$

$$p[P_c] = (p[G \Rightarrow C] + p[\sim C])/2 = (4 + 3)/2 = 3.50 \qquad (D.3)$$

So in this case one can see that the most plausible MCS, i.e., the one with the lowest plausibility index) is $P_b$. The meaning of this MCS is that the data and the counterclaim are accepted as true and the inference model is rejected. More complex decision-theoretic procedures can be formulated considering multiple sets and/or sources of data, different types of warrants, and multiple competing claims. An approach to handling the complex cases is to identify the least plausible portion of the argument and choose the most plausible policy from the set of conclusions derived from the MCSs. The gamut of possible assertions concerning a claim, data, and warrant is presented in Table D.2.

**TABLE D.2.**
**Assertions Concerning Grounds (G), Warrants (W) and Claims (C)**

| MCS Item | $P_a$ G,C | $P_b$ G,~C | $P_c$ ~G,C | $P_d$ ~G,~C | Logical symbol | Comment |
|---|---|---|---|---|---|---|
| 1 | 1 | 1 | 1 | 1 | Tautology | Tautolog |
| 2 | 1 | 1 | 1 | 0 | ~G $\Rightarrow$ C | Alternative warrant |
| 3 | 1 | 1 | 0 | 1 | ~G $\Rightarrow$ ~C | Alternative warrant |
| 4 | 1 | 1 | 0 | 0 | G | Grounds  *This is* |
| 5 | 1 | 0 | 1 | 1 | G $\Rightarrow$ C | Warrant  *the basic* |
| 6 | 1 | 0 | 1 | 0 | C | Claim  *argument* |
| 7 | 1 | 0 | 0 | 1 | (G $\wedge$ C) or (~G $\wedge$ ~C) | Assert specific state |
| 8 | 1 | 0 | 0 | 0 | ~(G $\Rightarrow$ ~C) | Alternative warrant |
| 9 | 0 | 1 | 1 | 1 | G $\Rightarrow$ ~C | Alternative warrant |
| 10 | 0 | 1 | 1 | 0 | (G $\wedge$ ~C) or (~G $\wedge$ C) | Assert the specific state |
| 11 | 0 | 1 | 0 | 1 | ~C | Deny the claim |
| 12 | 0 | 1 | 0 | 1 | ~(G $\Rightarrow$ C) | Alternative warrant |
| 13 | 0 | 0 | 1 | 1 | ~G | Deny the grounds |
| 14 | 0 | 0 | 1 | 0 | ~(~G $\Rightarrow$ ~C) | Alternative warrant |
| 15 | 0 | 0 | 0 | 1 | ~(~G $\Rightarrow$ C) | Alternative warrant |
| 16 | 0 | 0 | 0 | 0 | Irrelevant | Meaningless, irrelevant |

Since it is normal that there will be knowledge and arguments for both supporting and contradicting the claim, warrants, grounds, and rebuttals, the problem of
dealing with inconsistent portions of an argument is a general one. Using the
approach explained above, one can reduce the different kinds of rebuttals and their
corresponding MCSs to a tabular form and can compute the plausibilities of the
MCSs from simple formulas.

# About the Author

Charles L. Smith, Sr. has a Ph.D. in Information Technology from George Mason University in Fairfax, Virginia. He has worked for many companies in the space, defense, and commercial areas. All of his work has involved the use of computer technology for technical problem solving. He is currently in business for himself in Brunswick, Georgia. He was formerly an adjunct professor at the Florida Institute of Technology graduate school at their off-campus site in Alexandria, Virginia. He has three grown children and currently resides in Annandale, Virginia.

# Notes

[1]Where missed opportunities, or issues, and incorrect decisions can have a most deleterious effect on an organization.

[2]So that decisions are more often correct or the outcome is more beneficial to the user.

[3]Another form of DSS is called an Executive Information System (EIS), which is ostensibly for use by executives.

[4]Humanized computers have all the senses of a person.

[5]Issues that are ill-structured cannot be resolved using the methods of operations research, that is, one or more of the following is not known: the set of possible actions, the set of possible states of nature, the set of possible outcomes, or the set of utilities of the outcomes to the user.

[6]From information theory, an increase in information corresponds to an increase in entropy, and vice versa, where entropy (H) is always nonnegative and where $H = -\Sigma_i p_i \log_a p_i$ where $p_i$ is the probability of the $i^{th}$ event and usually a = 2 so that a basic element of information is a bit (i.e., a 0 or 1).

[7]As stated previously, this is more generally known as prognosis.

[8]That is, decide how to decide.

[9]Throughout this book the term "user" will mean either a decision maker or the user of a DSS.

[10]A system that attempts to adapt to its environment.

[11]Inquiring systems are beyond the scope of this book, but there are at least four of them: a) empirical, b) theoretical, c) empirical-theoretical, and d) dialectical (Churchman, 1971). These systems are methods for analyzing and evaluating hypothetical statements.

[12]The templates would consist of issue descriptions, with appropriate value ranges of the pertinent parameters, and appropriate responses should there be a match.

[13]Some of which perhaps can be automated.

[14]A change can be a deletion of, a modification to, or an addition of, an existing item.

[15]Widgets are the building blocks used to create a user interface. Some widgets have a specific appearance and behavior in the interface display. Examples of widgets include buttons, labels, and text fields. Another type of widget is invisible by itself, but serves to contain and organize other widgets. Examples include the form, bulletin board, menu bar, and row column widgets.

[16]When I say "take the user to screen . . . . " it can mean actually changing the entire viewing area on the PC or it can mean presenting the new viewing area as a small window embedded in the larger PC screen area.

[17]In many cases in this demonstration, the demo DSS could have been designed to use a listed set of predetermined alternatives, such as a menu list, to be used to identify the alternatives.

# References

Allison, G. (1971). *Essence of decision: Explaining the Cuban Missile Crisis.* Boston: Little, Brown and Company.

Andriole, S. (Ed.) (1986). *Microcomputer decision support systems.* Wellesley, MA: QED Information Sciences.

Apple Computer (1993). *HyperCard script language guide.* Cupertino, CA.

Argyris, C. (1982). *Reasoning, learning, and action: Individual and organizational.* San Francisco: Jossey-Bass.

Boar, B. (1993). *Implementing client/server computing.* New York: McGraw-Hill.

Bouwman, M. (1983). Human diagnostic reasoning by computer: An illustration from financial analysis. *Management Science, 29,* (6), 653–672.

Churchman, C. (1971). *The design of inquiring systems: Basic concepts of systems and organization.* New York: Basic Books.

Cohen, M., March, J., & Olsen, J. (1972). A garbage can model of organizational choice. *Administrative Science Quarterly, 17,* 1–25.

Covey, S. (1991). *Principle-centered leadership.* New York: Simon & Schuster.

Cowan, D. (1986). Developing a process model of problem recognition. *Academy of Management Review, 11,* (4), 763–776.

Dawes, R. (1979). The robust beauty of improper linear models in decision making. *American Psychologist, 34,* 571–582.

de Kleer, J. (1986). An assumption-based truth maintenance system. *Artificial Intelligence, 28,* 127–162.

Diesing, P. (1962). *Reason in society.* Urbana, IL: University of Illinois Press.

Doessel, D. (1986). Medical diagnosis as a problem in the economics of information. *Information Economics and Policy, 2,* 49–68.

Dolk, D. (1988). Model management and structured modeling: The role of an information resource dictionary system. *Communications of the ACM, 31,* (6), 704–716.

Dreyfus, H., & Dreyfus, S. (1980). A five stage model of the mental activities involved in directed skill acquisition. University of California at Berkeley, Rep. ORC 80-2.

Eisenhardt, K. (1989). Making fast strategic decisions in high-velocity environments. *Academy of Management Journal, 32,* (3), 543–576.

Eldred, E., & Sylvester, T. (1994). Two databases for modeling complex data without the oh-ohs. *Client/Server Today,* 67–72.

English, E. (1995, February). DSP could humanize computers. *IEEE Computer, 9.*

Etzioni, A. (1967). Mixed scanning: A third approach to decision making. *Public Administration Review*, *27*, 385–392.

Etzioni, A. (1968). *The active society, a theory of societal and political processes*. New York: The Free Press.

Evans, J. (1989). A review and synthesis of OR/MS and creative problem solving (Parts 1 and 2). *OMEGA International Journal of Management Science*, *17*, (6), 499–524.

Fischhoff, B. (1982). Debiasing. In D. Kahneman, P. Slovic, & A. Tversky, *Judgment under uncertainty: Heuristics and biases* (pp. 423–444). Cambridge, UK: Cambridge University Press.

Fishburn, P. (1970). *Utility theory for decision making*. New York: John Wiley and Sons.

Ford, J., Schmitt, N., Schechtman, S., Hults, B., & Doherty, M. (1989). Process tracing methods: Contributions, problems, and neglected research questions. *Organizational Behavior and Human Decisional Processes*, *43*, 75–117.

Gallupe, R., & DeSanctis, G. (1988). Computer-based support for group problem-finding: An experimental investigation. *MIS Quarterly*, 277–295.

Geoffrion, A. (1989). Computer-based modeling environments. *European Journal of Operational Research*, 41, 33–43.

Grudin, J. (1989). The case against user interface consistency. *Communications of the ACM*, *32*, (10), 1164–1173.

Hale, G. (1996). *The leader's edge, mastering the 5 skills of breakthrough thinking*. Burr Ridge, IL: Irwin Professional Publishing.

Hammer, M., & Champy, R. (1993). *Reengineering the corporation, a manifesto for business revolution*. New York: Harper Business.

Heninger, K. (1980). Specifying software requirements for complex systems: New techniques and their application. *IEEE Transactions of Software Engineering*, *SE-6*, (1), 2–13.

Heyer, P. (1966). *Architects on architecture, new directions in America*. New York: Walker and Company.

Hsia, P., Samuel, J., Gao, J., Kung, D., Toyoshima, Y., & Chen, C. (1994). Formal approach to scenario analysis. *IEEE SOFTWARE*, 33–41.

Hsia, P., Davis, A., & Kung, D. (1994, March). Response to a letter to the editor. *IEEE SOFTWARE*, pp. 8–9.

Huber, G. (1990). A theory of the effects of advanced information technologies on organizational design, intelligence, and decision making. *Academy of Management Review*, *15*, (1), 47–71.

Hurson, A., Pakzad, S., & Cheng, J. (1993). Object-oriented database management systems: Evolution and performance issues. *IEEE COMPUTER*, 48–60.

Institute of Electrical and Electronic Engineers (1984). *The IEEE guide to software requirements specifications*. ANSI/IEEE Standard #830-1984. New York: The Institute of Electrical and Electronic Engineers.

Janis, I., & Mann, L. (1977). *Decision making: A psychological analysis of conflict, choice, and commitment*. New York: The Free Press.

Khoshafian, S., & Abnous, R. (1990). *Object orientation*. New York: John Wiley & Sons.

Lindblom, C. (1959). The science of "muddling through." *Public Administration Review*, *19*, 155–169.

Lindland, O., Sindre, G., & Solvberg, A. (1994, March). Understanding quality in conceptual modeling. *IEEE SOFTWARE*.

Linstone, H. (1984). *Multiple perspectives for decision making*. Amsterdam: North-Holland.

Mason, R., & Mitroff, I. (1981). *Challenging strategic planning assumptions: Theory, cases, and techniques*. New York: John Wiley & Sons.

McCain, G., & Segal, E. (1988). *The game of science*. Pacific Grove, CA: Brooks/Cole.

McKeeney, J., & Keen, P. (1974). How managers' "minds work." *Harvard Business Review*, 52, (3), 79–90.

MicroStrategy (1995a). *DSS agent brochure*.

MicroStrategy (1995b). *True relational OLAP brochure*.

Moravec, H. (1995). An intoxicating idea (again). *IEEE Spectrum, 12*.

Morgan, M. (Translator). (1914). *Vitruvius, the ten books of architecture*. New York: Dover Publications.

Naisbitt, J. (1984). *Megatrends*. New York: Warner Books.

Nesbitt, R., Krantz, D., Jepson, C., & Fong, G. (1982). Improving inductive inference. In D. Kahneman, P. Slovic, & A. Tversky, *Judgment under uncertainty: Heuristics and biases* (pp. 445–459). Cambridge, UK: Cambridge University Press.

Noble, D. (1987). Template-based data fusion for situation assessment. *Data Fusion Symposium 1987*, 156–161.

*Open software foundation style guide* (1993). Englewood Cliffs, NJ: Prentice-Hall.

Paulk, M., Weber, C., Garcia, S., Chrissis, M., & Bush, M. (1993a). *Key practices of the capability maturity model, Version 1.1*. CMU/SEI-93-TR-25.

Paulk, M., Curtis, B., Chrissis, M., & Weber, C. (1993b). *Capability maturity model for software, Version 1.1*. CMU/SEI-93-TR-24.

Peters, T. (1987). *Thriving on chaos*. New York: HarperCollins.

Prigogine, I., & Stengars, I. (1984). *Order out of chaos: Man's new dialogue with nature*. New York: Bantam Books.

Radford, K. (1990). The strategic/tactical model for resolution of complex decision situations (SANTA). *Information and Decision Technologies, 16*, 333–346.

Raiffa, H. (1970). *Decision analysis, introductory lectures on choices under uncertainty*. Reading, MA: Addison-Wesley.

Rasmussen, J. (1980). Models of mental strategies in process plant diagnosis. In *NATO symposium on human detection and diagnosis of system failures* (pp. 241–258). New York: Plenum Press.

Rasmussen, J. (1986). *Information processing and human-machine interaction: An approach to cognitive engineering*. New York: North-Holland.

Rasmussen, J., & Vicente, K. (1989). Coping with human errors through system design: Implications for ecological interface design. *International Journal of Man-Machine Studies, 31*, 517–534.

Reason, J. (1987). Generic error modeling system (GEMS): A cognitive framework for locating common human error forms. In J. Rasmussen, K. Duncan, & J. Leplat (Eds.), *New technology and human error*, (pp. 63–83). Chichester, UK: John Wiley & Sons.

Rencken, W., & Durrant-Whyte, H. (1993). A quantitative model for adaptive task allocation in human-computer interfaces. *IEEE Transactions of Systems, Man, and Cybernetics, 23*, (4), 1062–1071.

Sage, A. (1977). *Methodology for large-scale systems*. New York: McGraw-Hill.

Sage, A. (1981). Behavioral and organizational considerations in the design of information systems and processes for planning and decision support. *IEEE Transactions on Systems, Man, and Cybernetics, 11*, (9), 640–678.

Sage, A. (Ed.) (1990). *Concise encyclopedia of information processing in systems and organizations.* Oxford, UK: Pergamon Press.

Sage, A. (1992a). *Decision support systems engineering.* New York: John Wiley & Sons.

Sage, A. (1992b). *Systems engineering.* New York: John Wiley & Sons.

Sage, A., & Palmer, J. (1990). *Software systems engineering.* New York: John Wiley & Sons.

Sage, A., & White, E. (1983). Decision and information structures in regret models of judgment and choice. *IEEE Transactions on Systems, Man, and Cybernetics, SMC-13*, (3), 136–144.

Schum, D. (1987). *Evidence and inference for the intelligence analyst, I & II.* Lanham, MD: University Press of America.

Shortliffe, E. (1976). *Computer based medical consultation: MYCIN.* New York: American Elsevier.

Slovic, P., Fischhoff, B., & Lichtenstein, S. (1982). Facts versus fears: Understanding perceived risk. In D. Kahneman, P. Slovic, & A. Tversky, *Judgment under uncertainty: Heuristics and biases* (pp. 463–489). Cambridge, UK: Cambridge University Press.

Simon, H. (1972). Theories of bounded rationality. In C. Radner & R. Radner (Eds.), *Method and appraisal* (pp. 161–176). Cambridge, UK: North-Holland.

Smith, Sr., C. (1992). *A theory of situation assessment for decision support.* PhD Dissertation, George Mason University, Fairfax, VA.

Smith, Sr., C., Morgan, P., & Wilson, A. (1994). *Information System Upgrade Requirements Independent Assessment Report.* Lanham, MD: IITRI Informal Report.

Smith, Sr., C., & Sage, A. (1989). Systems management of technology infusion and new product development. *Information and Decision Technologies, 15*, 343–358.

Smith, S., & Mosier, J. (1986). *Guidelines for designing user interface software.* The MITRE Corporation, MTR 10090.

Sprague, R., & Carlson, E. (1982). *Building effective decision support systems.* Englewood Cliffs, NJ: Prentice-Hall.

Toulmin, S. (1958). *The uses of argument.* Cambridge, UK: Cambridge University Press.

Toulmin, S., Reike, R., & Janik, A. (1979). *An introduction to reasoning.* New York: Macmillan.

Turban, E. (1990). *Decision support and expert systems.* New York: Macmillan.

von Neumann, J., & Morgenstern, O. (1953). *Theory of games and economic behavior.* New York: John Wiley & Sons.

Wohl, J. (1981). Force management and decision requirements for Air Force tactical command and control. *IEEE Transactions on Systems, Man, and Cybernetics, SMC-11*, (9), 618–639.

# Author Index

# Subject Index